Personal Leadership:
Taking Control of Your Work Life

BY JOHN BALDONI

Personal Leadership:
Taking Control of Your Work Life

© 2001 John Baldoni

The author is grateful to the following authors for permission to quote from their published works:

Jill Ker Conway *The Road to Coorain*
Conway, Jill Ker *Road from Coorain.* New York: Alfred Knopf 1989

Gordon Sullivan *Hope is Not a Method*
Sullivan, Gordon R. and Harper, Michael V. *Hope is Not a Method.* New York: Times Books 1996

Elsewhere Press
1326 Gettysburg
Rochester Hills, MI 48306
www.elsewherepress.com

ISBN: 0-9657345-1-X

Library of Congress Card Number: 00-191299

Table of Contents

PART I: HOW I CAN LEAD
Putting Leadership into Practice

PART II: HOW OTHERS LEAD
Stories from the Front Lines of Leadership

*Leadership is the art of
influencing human behavior.*

U.S. ARMY PUBLICATION (1948)

Prologue

Have you been:

- Promoted to your first management position?
- Selected to head a volunteer organization?
- Named to a new coaching position?
- Elected to the school board?
- Asked to turn a team of talented individuals into your company's next generation of leadership?
- Advised by a close friend to be more assertive?
- Interested in what makes a good leader?

If so, this book has been written for you.

The challenge you are facing now is the one that every leader has faced. How you meet this challenge will determine your effectiveness as a leader. Some of us may build a company, run for political office, discover a scientific breakthrough, coach a team, but even if we do none of those things, we can still lead.

Why? Because leadership begins with the individual!

If we want a better company, better schools, better society, we must exert a degree of personal leadership. Just what is personal leadership? In a nutshell, it is a matter of exerting personal autonomy, personal initiative, and personal responsibility. Personal leadership involves moving from the "I can" to the "I will." The purpose of this book is to help you make that move.

Personal Leadership: Taking Charge of Your Work Life will be your action planner to leadership development. It is my belief that all of us have the potential to be leaders; we simply need to be shown the way. Personal leadership is grounded in personal beliefs and core values. It is essential that a leader lead himself before he can lead others.

In this book you will meet a group of extraordinary leaders who guide organizations both large and small based upon the principles found in this book. These leaders include:

- Jac Nasser, CEO and president, Ford Motor Company
- Red Berenson, University of Michigan two-time NCAA championship hockey coach
- Jill Ker Conway, author and former president of Smith College
- Skip LeFauve, retired president of Saturn Corporation
- Janette Jackson, elementary school principal
- David McKinnon, CEO, Molly Maid
- Rick Snyder, president, Avalon Investments
- Members of the Wolverine Battalion, U.S. Army
- Eleanor Josaitis, executive director of the nonprofit service agency, Focus: HOPE

All of them learned to lead themselves before they led others.

As always, there is a desperate need for leadership in our lives. When times are good, we want a firm hand on the tiller to keep our ship running with the wind. When times are bad, we want someone to grab the tiller and swing our ship around into the wind.

Of course this scenario is simply a metaphor. Times are never wholly good, nor wholly bad, usually one part or the other dominates. For example, in a robust economy, there are pockets of incorrigible poverty and still way too much violence. Likewise, during poor economic times, there are those who profit handsomely and those whose giving enriches the lives of others.

The truth of the matter is that the pendulum between fortune and misfortune swings regularly. It is an indicator of the change process. The only constant in our lives is, indeed, change.

Consider:

- *In Technology.* Rapid advancements have altered time and distance to a degree that we now live in what author Regis McKenna calls "real time"—a compressed period where time and space merge in a new dimension.[1]

- *In Sports.* Remember when your home team had players you knew by name? Today the roster changes from day to day. "Who's on First?" has never had more meaning.

- *In Fashion.* In the office, men and women dressed in suits. Today we wear what we want to wear. In some places, jeans are considered "dress up."

- *In Athletic Wear.* Tennis shoes were something you wore to play the sport. Today athletic shoes with stripes, streaks or swooshes to suit your taste are appropriate for nearly every occasion.

- *In Education.* Kids "learned" what they were told to "learn." Today children explore new horizons and take teachers along for the ride.

- *In Products.* Once manufacturers produced what they wanted; today savvy manufacturers build to order.

- *In Customer Approach.* Once customers were considered children—to be seen but not heard. Today companies fall all over themselves to get the customer to make decisions for them.

- *In Management.* From the dawn of the Industrial Age to the 1970s, hierarchy was the watchword of American Industry. The military system of top-down management was the ideal model. Even the U.S. Army encourages participatory decision-making...as do most forward-thinking organizations.

- *In Social Norms.* Remember when what we saw on *Ozzie & Harriet* seemed the family ideal. Today's kids take their cues from *Bevis and Butthead.* The "in your face" smarminess is celebrated as a rite of passage. (Ahhhh!!!!)

- *In Society.* We baby boomers thought we broke conventions, but Generation Xers are taking our values and replacing them with their own ideas about work, family, and our future.

We live in a time that historian Daniel Boorstein calls the "fertile verge"—a convergence of new technologies and new approaches are changing society forever. A symptom of convergence is acceleration, things are happening around us and to us at an ever-increasing rate.

We, therefore, cannot ignore change, nor even endure it. We must embrace it. But how? How will we choose the right path?

Well, as an optimist, I say we will choose the right leaders—in business, politics, education, and religion—that will point us in the right direction. But again, is this realistic? Why are we waiting for someone else to step forward?

Why not us? You and me!

It is my firm hope that readers will take the information in this book and find it useful, today, tomorrow, or at some future date. The way you interpret and use this information is what will be unique. No two individuals will use what they find in these pages in exactly the same manner. But ideally both will find value in these ideas.

The structure of *Personal Leadership* is easy to scan and easy to reference. The book is divided into two sections covering theory and practice.

Part One: How I Can Lead

Part One includes a selection of *Leadership Essays* covering different aspects of the leadership process. These include:

- Character
- Vision
- Strategy
- Time Management
- Communications
- Recognition
- Emotional Intelligence
- Change Leadership
- Reflection
- Supervision

To make the material more accessible and understandable, each essay will feature a simple graphic illustration. These models will help the reader navigate the material as well as serve as a handy guide for future reference.

At the close of each *Leadership Essay* are *Leadership Exercises:* Ultimately the success of this book depends upon you and your participation. There is a self-assessment at the close of each chapter to measure your current abilities in key leadership areas. Also included is an action planner containing exercises to help you improve your leadership skills.

Part Two: How Others Lead
Stories from the Front Lines of Leadership

Part Two contains nine *Leadership Profiles*. The real-life leaders, who range from CEOs and Executive Directors to coaches and school principals, make the lessons of leadership accessible and practical. Their examples of leadership in action provide insight into what it takes to be a leader.

The blend of anecdote and personal example, combined with theory and practice, will enable you to begin to develop new leadership skills, or refine current ones, in ways that will help you lead yourself, and ultimately others.

Personal Leadership will help you put your own hand on the "tiller" to navigate the seas of change in ways that benefit yourself and others. Ultimately, this book will be your guide to developing a leadership style that resonates with authority, insight, and understanding—in other words, leadership. Happy leading!

PART **1**
How I Can Lead

A selection of Leadership Essays covering different aspects of the leadership process.

Enlightened leadership is service,
not selfishness.

JOHN HEIDER

CHAPTER 1

What is Personal Leadership?

Leadership is an active, living process. It is rooted in character, forged by experience, and communicated by example.

Management theorists posit many views of leadership. But many overlook the need for personal leadership, which I define as self-confidence backed by conviction and understanding. Another term might be "personal mastery"—knowing where you stand, where you want to go, and what you need to sacrifice to get there. Whatever you call it, personal leadership stems from one's core beliefs and values and is essential to leading others.

Here are some examples of personal leadership:

- Leadership is a young woman just beginning her career who spots a problem within her team, and takes it upon herself to correct it.
- Leadership is when the manager of one team approaches his counterpart in another and initiates a conversation about how the teams might cooperate to meet a common goal.
- Leadership is the manager who makes an effort to get to know his staff by holding occasional meetings with no agenda. He facilitates dialogue in order to solicit what's on the minds of his direct reports.
- Leadership is a manager who takes the time to "teach" his people, new and old, the norms of his organization and his expectations of and for his people.

In each of these examples, the manager-leader demonstrates personal mastery; she does not wait to be told. She sizes up a situation and does what is necessary to help her people do the job, and contribute more effectively.

There is no "man on a white horse" in any of these examples. Just leaders grounded in common sense who know how to get the job done.

Effective management today is less and less about "managing," i.e., administering. Effective management is about leadership, exerting personal initiative that stems from personal vision, a sense that "I know what needs to be done, and I will do it." Effective management stems from core values that shape a personal leadership style.

What Personal Leadership Is *Not*

When defining a topic that can be as elusive as personal leadership, it can seem as daunting as swimming across a large lake. The topic is so broad and so deep that once you dive into it you can quickly get over your head flailing away at concepts that seem relevant academically, but irrelevant personally.

So let's drain some of the water by declaring what leadership is not.

"Leadership is not hitting someone over the head," Dwight Eisenhower once said. "That's assault." [1] Raising your voice and shouting does not engender respect. It may generate fear, but it does little to enhance personal dignity of the worker. Yet many managers in leadership positions like to rule by fear. How many times have you heard a manager say, "I need to yell. It's the only way to get things done"? Sure, yelling might stimulate an employee to continue working, but it certainly will not encourage him to contribute anymore than the minimum effort. Shouting says, "I'm in charge, you're not, so do what I say."

Raising your voice is symptomatic of the traditional labor-management relationship, one that is based upon autocratic rule. It fosters a "do as you're told" mentality. The manager sets the objective and the worker fulfills it without question. The command-and-control approach can work well for a centralized, growth market where high-volume production is required. But when the market fractionalizes into many decentralized segments, the command-and-control model becomes an obstacle because it does not permit ideas to flow from any other source but the top.

In today's economy we have many hundreds of multi-segment markets, each with its own competing demands. Therefore, we need a new model of management, one that encourages participation. Why? Because in a market with competing needs, it is the person on the front lines who often knows more about the customer and his needs than some executive sitting in a central office. If the company is to survive, it must encourage ideas that flow upward as well as downward.

The concept in many leading companies is empowerment, letting employees and workers determine their own objectives and thereby exert a level of accountability in job design, execution, and fulfillment. Empowerment is another word for personal leadership, but a type of individual leadership that requires participation of both leader and follower. Both individuals must exert personal autonomy, initiative, and responsibility. [Unfortunately, the word "empowerment" has fallen from grace in certain companies because it was never practiced properly: managers did not cede any decision-making and employees felt ignored. As a result both managers and employees view it as a kind of "flavor of the month" that is past its due date.]

What Personal Leadership *Is*

Those three words—autonomy, initiative, and responsibility—form the essence of what personal leadership truly is.

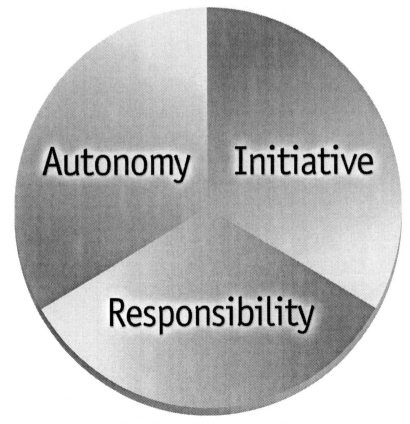

Key Drivers of Personal Leadership

Autonomy is the willingness to lead others. It is a driving force behind leadership because autonomy is the inner drive that pushes a leader forward. For example, when Cincinnatus, the citizen-farmer of Rome, stepped forward to lead his people in time of need, he was answering the call of leadership. He was willing to assume command, to be autonomous. Similarly men and women in management positions aspire to move up the organizational ladder to assume more authority. They are exercising autonomy.

Initiative is the willingness to take action, to make something happen. Without initiative, there is inertia. A leader's responsibility is to move people, either physically or ideologically, so the leader herself must have an inner need to move, too. Some define this characteristic as being a "self-starter." The term is an apt one because it indicates a desire to create. Initiative also is the key motivator of the entrepreneur. Entrepreneurs are those individuals who look for possibilities where others see closed doors. Initiative is the inner drive that says, "Yes, I can make it happen."

Responsibility is the willingness to be accountable for consequences. "Success has many fathers, but failure is an orphan" was a favorite saying of John F. Kennedy. So it is with responsibility. When a project exceeds expectations, it's easy to take credit. When the project tanks, it takes a measure of character to assume responsibility. Leadership is built upon responsibility; without it there is no leadership.

Autonomy, initiative, and responsibility work hand-in-glove to form the essential elements of personal leadership. These elements act as drivers of leadership transforming it from something that is to something that does.

How to Exert a Willingness to Lead

Personal leadership is first and foremost "personal." It stems from your beliefs. And here are a few traits that I have observed from leaders I know personally, as well as those I know by reputation.

Personal Leadership Is Centered

One cannot lead others if he does not know his own mind. Being centered implies having a sense of grounding. This grounding may come from education, from faith in God, or from family. Centeredness and knowing oneself gives a leader the confidence she needs to lead others.

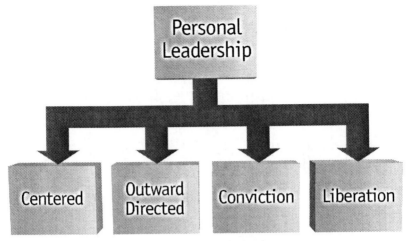

The Leadership Process

Personal Leadership Is Outward

Leaders who know themselves can lead others. Leadership is the art and practice of moving people from one place to another. Most often the place is not a location, but an aspiration—a better place for body, mind, and spirit. As such it is directed outward and requires the participation of followers.

Personal Leadership Is Steeled By the Courage of Conviction

As with centeredness, courage is essential. All of us, at one time or another, must take a stand on uncomfortable issues. Where you stand can determine the course of a project, the future of a new application, or the direction of a new marketing initiative. It takes a strong person to impose his will and stick with it. Courage of conviction, however, is not to be confused with bull-headedness. A good leader knows the difference, or at least is wise enough to listen to trusted individuals who tell him so.

Personal Leadership Is Liberating

The leader who can look outward, yet is secure within himself, is freed himself from second-guessing himself. Often the most important service a leader can do is to delegate responsibility. A leader should be able to stand back and let her people do their jobs. Personal leadership liberates the individual and the team to fulfill their own potential.

Leadership by definition grows and expands with the individual. Leadership is a matter of taking personal responsibility for oneself, as well as collective responsibility for others, enabling everyone in the organization to grow and improve.

Defining Leadership
Character

Supervising and
Leading Others

Creating
Leadership Vision

Reflecting on
Leadership

**Personal
Leadership**

Developing
Leadership
Strategy

Learning to
be a Change
Leader

Maximizing
Time to Lead

Demonstrating
Leadership
Emotions

Communicating
Leadership

Recognizing the
Contributions of
Others

Cycle of Personal Leadership

Ten Elements of Personal Leadership

Leadership is ultimately an active process. One leads, others follow. Leadership involves movement, going from one place, or state of being to another. It is about engaging the drivers of autonomy, initiative, and responsibility in ways to make things happen.

There are ten aspects to Personal Leadership:

1. Character
2. Vision
3. Strategy
4. Time Management
5. Communications
6. Recognition
7. Leadership Emotions
8. Change Leadership
9. Reflection
10. Supervision

Some of these aspects are directed inwardly toward the self; others are directed outwardly toward others. All of them, however, work together to create a cycle of leadership behaviors that nurtures the leadership process. Personal leadership is the process of doing and in the act of doing it creates a momentum that pulls others forward along with the leader.

Effective leadership works because the leader, as historian and leadership philosopher James MacGregor Burns has written, taps into the inner dreams and aspirations of the followers.[2] Good leadership encourages followership because good leadership affirms the follower's own personal values. Often what happens is the leader awakens the follower's own strong reserve of character and value. Some followers may not realize they hold such values until the right leader taps into them and mobilizes them to action. For example, followers of Martin Luther King felt better about themselves when they listened to his moving eloquence. But more importantly, King awakened within his followers a spirit of social justice, which gave them the courage to take up his cause despite great danger. [It must be acknowledged that evil leaders, such as Hitler or Stalin, can stir dark passions within their followers, too. It is a form of leadership, but it is one that calls for the subjugation of others and as such is inherently wrong.]

What This Book is About

The remaining chapters in Part One will demonstrate how you can develop your own personal leadership abilities in order to become a more effective leader.

Defining Leadership Character

Leadership character, which is the sum of strong morals as well as compassion, conviction and integrity, provides the leader with the strength to lead.

Creating a Leadership Vision

Vision is the sense of personal mission. Vision is the "Where do you want to go?" and "Why do you want to go there?" It frames a leader's intentions and reasons for leadership.

Developing a Leadership Strategy

Strategy is the means of getting from here to there. It puts the vision into action. Strategy also serves as the personal "call to action." When issued, strategy acts to marshal resources, internal and external, to fulfill the vision.

Maximizing Time to Lead

A leader's most precious resource is time. If used correctly, time can be the enabler of greatness. It can permit the leader to achieve goals individually and collectively. But, like gold, it must be managed wisely.

Communicating Leadership

Communication is the glue that holds an organization together. Communication involves words, actions, thoughts, and deeds. Knitting these elements together is the willingness to listen to others.

Recognizing the Contributions of Others

No leader can accomplish goals alone. It requires followership. Those followers need to be recognized for their contributions. Recognition is the "pat on the back" that says you are doing a good job. It is an affirmation of individual and collective character.

Demonstrating Leadership Emotions

What we consider as intelligence is an amalgam of cognitive, affective, and social skills. Of these, the ability to know oneself as well as the ability to get along with others are essential to effective leadership. The leader who is balanced inside will be "well-balanced" outside, and thereby have the capacity to inspire confidence and trust.

Learning to be a Change Leader

Leaders are called upon to guide people through change. To do so effectively, the leader must anticipate, manage, and embrace change as well as commit to a continuous learning process in preparation for change.

Reflecting on Leadership

Leadership naturally invites criticism from others. It is the mark of a good leader to learn from mistakes. Part of the learning process involves a willingness to examine the inner self. We call it reflection. It is a process that those who practice is find indispensable to their ability to lead.

Supervising and Leading Others

Supervision is the leadership of others. It requires the application of virtually every leadership attribute and behavior. Supervision involves both the setting of expectations as well as the release of hands-on control. Bottom line, effective supervision is leadership in action.

Self-Assessment: Elements of Personal Leadership

Leadership is rooted in personal commitment and a desire to benefit others. Use this assessment to evaluate your opinions about personal leadership.

Personal Leadership Assessment					
1. Leaders lead by personal example.	①	②	③	④	⑤
2. Having a set of personal principles is important to leadership.	①	②	③	④	⑤
3. If do not know the answer to an important question, I am willing to search for an answer.	①	②	③	④	⑤
4. When something goes wrong, I look to make it right.	①	②	③	④	⑤
5. Knowing where you want to go is important to leadership.	①	②	③	④	⑤
6. I want to make those around me succeed.	①	②	③	④	⑤

1—*Strongly Disagree*   2—*Disagree*   3—*Neutral*
4—*Agree*   5—*Strongly Agree*

Rate Yourself

If you scored between…

26–30   Excellent leadership skills
25–20   Good leadership abilities
19–15   Learning to lead
 >15   Need improvement

Note: *If you evaluate yourself as you read each of the leadership chapters (1–11), you will develop an overall picture of yourself as a leader. If you re-take the same evaluations after you begin to practice some of the leadership behaviors noted in the book, you may notice real improvement in your assessment of your leadership skills.*

Action Planner: Planning to Lead

You can look at leadership as the art and practice of getting things done with the best intentions of your followers in mind. Take a moment to answer these questions. Jot down your answers. If you don't know the answer right away, come back and answer it later. The important thing is to reflect. From reflection, emerges perspective. And perspective is critical to leadership.

Reflective Questions

1. Consider the best teacher you ever had.

   • What were his/her qualities that made him/her a good teacher?

   • How did this teacher capture your attention?

   • What did this teacher do to make the material come alive?

2. Reflect on a leader in your personal experience.

   • What were his/her qualities that you admire most?

   • How did this person influence you?

   • What can you learn from this individual?

3. List some ways you can be more accountable.

   • To your peers

   • To your spouse

   • To your family

4. Consider ways you can demonstrate initiative.

   • At work

   • At home

5. Think about ways to assume more responsibility.

   • At work

   • At home

   • In your community

6. Consider some ways you can begin to demonstrate personal leadership?

   • At work

   • At home

*Be more concerned with your character than
your reputation. Character is what you really are.
Reputation is what people say you are.*

JOHN WOODEN

CHAPTER 2
Defining Leadership Character

Leaders: Born or Bred?

Are leaders born or are they bred? Is there something within an individual's heritage that destines him to assume a leadership position? Or is leadership something that we learn from experience? You can make the argument that many fine leaders had families and educations that molded them to lead. Conversely, you can find leaders who came from dire straits and rose to leadership through hard work and enterprise.

Character to Lead

To answer the question of born or bred, we need to explore the leadership character of an individual. What is leadership character? I define it as a sum of personal integrity and moral values. Leadership lacking these traits is like a made-for-display wedding cake. It may look good, but underneath the decorative icing is cardboard. Leadership character is the reflection of the inner self. While the external self may be scarred and pitted from years of hard knocks, the inner self remains vigorous, vibrant, and resilient. [By contrast, those who rule by fear lack integrity and positive values; therefore, they do not possess leadership character.]

Leadership character, however, is not perfection. All of us make mistakes, some minor, some major. Character gives us the insight to know which is which, i.e., right from wrong. Often leadership character stems from redemption. The story of St. Paul is a marvelous example. As Paul of Tarsus, he was an ardent persecutor of Christians; after his conversion, as Paul the Apostle, he was die-hard promoter of the Faith.

Leadership character also may result from crisis. A case in point is Harry Truman. Thrust into the Presidency after the death of Franklin Roosevelt, Truman was suddenly propelled into a leadership role not merely of the United States, but of the world engaged in the last stages of World War II. It is true that Truman was not informed of the atomic bomb project, but it is not fair to assume, as his biographer David McCullough points out, that Truman was ill-prepared for the Presidency.[1]

His strength of character prepared him for any challenge he would face. That character was formed in his hard-scrabble days as a poor farmer in Missouri, as a struggling haberdasher in Kansas City, a seasoned combat officer in World War I. While Truman had never strode the world stage prior to his Presidency, he had passed through many character-building events that had forged him into a man of courage, integrity, and compassion ready for his turn in the spotlight.

A Matter of Leadership Character

So why is character important to leadership?

The answer is likely as simple or as complex as you wish to make it. A behaviorist might lecture for an entire course on the essence of character. A novelist can craft a 500-page novel based upon inner character. As for me, I'll stick with the short answer.

Character, to my way of thinking, is the essence of an individual. It is the reflection of the soul, the sense of depth that one conveys. Character emerges from personal values and beliefs. [By extension, the culture of an organization is the sum of its norms, behaviors, and values. In other words, its character.]

Character, of course, can be good or evil; or as with most of us, more good, but tinged with some darkness. Dramatists love the dark stuff because it invokes conflict with others and that discord is the heart of all dramatic interplay. By contrast, leadership character is good; it is human-centered leadership rooted in goodness. [Arguably, dictators get things accomplished, but their methods are coercion, torture, and death. Not the sort of model we would want to emulate.]

Personal Values Shape Leadership Character

Personal values are a reflection of cultural morals. Most religions of the world stem from the concept of a supernatural being whose life or example teaches us to aspire to goodness and service to others. Whether or not you ascribe divine qualities to the goodness is a matter of religious faith. Believers may argue all goodness stems from God. Humanists argue that goodness is a reflection of man's inner self.

Parents, teachers, and mentors teach values to the next generation. Very importantly, they bring the values to life through personal example and storytelling. In doing so, they make the values meaningful. They validate these values, which over time, the child may emulate as he grows up. Good values shape good leadership character—a willingness to do good for others. Of course, this is not the sole value, but I believe it is the core value from which respect of family, tradition, and others results.

Franklin Roosevelt is an example of someone whose family and circumstance both contributed to his leadership character. He was born into a patrician family and taught to care for the less fortunate as a matter of noblisse obligé. When polio crippled him for life he suddenly became one of the "less fortunate." Instead of pitying himself he turned his aristocratic outwardness to genuine empathy for others. As one of the afflicted, he was acutely conscious of the situations and plights of others. This understanding shaped his personal commitment toward helping others.

Conviction Drives Decisions

From personal values comes conviction. Conviction is the willingness to abide by a set of values, no matter what the cost. Conviction is a sort of last stand of what an individual will or will not do. Conviction shapes behavior. For a child, conviction may mean turning away from a friend who offers a cigarette. For a teen, it may be a refusal to climb into a car with someone who as been drinking. Conviction leads to positive choices. For an adult, conviction may be a decision to run for school board in order to make meaningful change.

Conviction is that inner voice that says, "Yes, I will do this because it is the right thing to do." Is conviction the same as conscience? Perhaps, but not exclusively. Conviction is formed by the set of values that are acted upon, usually toward a goal or for others. Conscience is inner directed. Conscience guides conviction, but does not prescribe it. Conviction is the will to make good happen. How? Through good decision-making. Conviction steels the will so that the leader can make the hard decision, one that may cause short-term pain, but long-term gain.

Hard decisions may be a choice between right and right, writes Joseph Badaracco, a professor of business ethics at the Harvard Business School.[2] Ethical decisions arise from making a choice between good or evil. What happens when there may be two right choices? For example, should a son make a business trip, or stay home to look after his hospitalized mother?

The trip may be important to the future of his company and its many employees. On the other hand, the man has only one mother.

Badaracco characterizes such dilemmas as "defining moments" that compel individuals to create a sense of balance between heart and home. While these moments may be emotionally wrenching, they create the opportunity for "personal growth."[3] In the long run, these moments of personal decision-making may be liberating because they free the individual to go forward in the knowledge that he has made the right decision.

The pain of the decision-making process defines the character of the individual. It may not make the next decision any easier. We do, however, expect our leaders to make the hard decisions. We may disagree with the outcome, but we nonetheless expect a decision to be made. By extension, we come to rely upon their judgment, their ability to discern what is best for the organization.

Leadership Character and the Change Process

This raises another question: what role does leadership character play in the change process?

Most of us are reluctant to disrupt the status quo. As human beings we crave stability; it is part of our nature that no doubt stems from our ancestral time as hunter-gathers huddled in caves safe from the elements and fierce animals. Yet then as now, sometimes you have to leave the cave. Leaders are the ones that go first; they are the ones seeking the new grasslands just over the next range. Their recognition of the right time to change is seated in leadership character, a willingness to do good for the organization.

Is a corporate executive who makes the decision to abandon a sagging market segment in favor of a potential new market, much different from an ancient tribal chieftain who sought better hunting grounds? Aside from some computer projections and reams of market data, probably not. We would like to think both leaders act for the good of the "tribe." Ideally, leaders should be change agents; their antennae are tuned to the winds of change so that we expect them to sense its importance before the rest of us and act accordingly.

Compassion for Others

This willingness to do good for people stems from their sense of compassion. Leaders need compassion. A leader who is not concerned with the welfare of those he leads is not a true leader. Again, to revisit Harry Truman, David McCullough says that he interviewed more than 100 people for his biography on the President. No one had anything negative to say about Truman's character with regard to treatment of others. Truman was a genuine man of the people, particularly the common people. Why? Because he was one of them and never pretended to be anything else. He was as sincere to the servants of the White House as he was to Heads of State.[4] [No doubt Truman liked some of his staff a whole heck of a lot better than many potentates.]

Compassion is a virtue, certainly. Leaders need volumes of it. Leaders cannot be "buddy-buddy" with their followers. Leaders can, and must, maintain a certain distance in order to make the tough decisions that will benefit the entire organization. In this equation, friendships suffer; how often is it that an executive may have to let go a personal friend because the friend is not doing right by the organization. That decision may cause the leader real pain, but he must do it for the good of the organization.

Leadership character includes our human frailties. Just as we are the sum of our strengths, we are also shaped by our weaknesses. It is this combination that makes us who we are. Our good side exists side-by-side in tension with our dark side. In public life, this tension is almost a cliché. You can think of many effective leaders who did much good but whose personal lives were tainted or marred by baser instincts: bribery, graft, and illicit sex. The same balance between good and evil resides in those outside the public eye. It is a matter of personal growth that we recognize our "dark side" and while not accommodating it, at least, learn to forgive ourselves if we fail to live up to our own personal standards.

Laughing at Ourselves

John F. Kennedy, who certainly had experiences with his "dark side," found relief in humor. One of his favorite saying concerned three key elements: God, human folly, and humor. Of the first two, man can do nothing about; of the third, it makes life bearable. Why?

Humor is a release, a chuckle at life's absurdities. Humor is a recognition of man's fallibility, our foibles and mistakes. But it is also fun. Humor is the everyday trip to the fun zone; it makes us laugh. John Cleese, the wickedly funny English comedian, believes that laughter is good for thinking because "when people laugh, it is easier for them to admit new ideas to their minds."[5] Trainers use humor to point out negative behaviors in ways that teach rather than preach. This notion is something that Cleese has pursued vigorously and hilariously with his series of humorous management videos.

Humor also is a means of releasing tension in the pressure-cooker atmosphere that sometimes engulfs us. Mediators tell us that the right joke, or the right moment of levity, can reduce tensions to the point that two adversaries can sit down at the table to consider the possibility of agreement. Leadership requires a good guffaw. Not only does it dissipate the tension of the moment, it makes others feel at ease, and likely more disposed to follow their leader.

Leaders need humor, I believe, to confirm their humanity. Franklin Roosevelt was known to relish daily doses of humor, typically during the cocktail hour. Does this mean that as President during the Great Depression and World War II, he was insensitive to the plight of the nation and its people? Quite the opposite. Joking in the face of crisis or tragedy is an affirmation of one's humanity. Laughing says "I am human, and therefore I, too, care about other human beings."

Are Leaders Born or Bred?

Leadership character then is the sum of personal values, conviction, and compassion, leavened with humor. But we may ask, does this equation result from birth or must it be learned? In other words, are leaders born or are they made?

I believe both. Some are destined to lead others. Teddy Roosevelt was born to lead other men. So was his cousin Franklin. By contrast, Harry Truman never aspired to leadership as a boy; he was working too hard to make a living to project too far into the future. Yet when the opportunity arose, he seized it and served himself and his nation well.

Destiny, of course, plays a role. In crisis leadership, destiny produces great men and women. In everyday terms, absent some crisis, leadership may be nurtured from circumstance and role-modeling. Frankly, it does not really matter from where leadership comes, what matters is the character of that leadership. And that stems from morals, values and integrity.

Self-Assessment: Elements of Leadership Character

Character based upon moral values is integral to leadership. Use this assessment to see how you rate your own leadership character.

Leadership Character Assessment					
1. I use my personal values as a basis of leadership.	①	②	③	④	⑤
2. My subordinates think I possess strong moral leadership.	①	②	③	④	⑤
3. I am willing to stand up for my principles even when it may hurt my chances for promotion.	①	②	③	④	⑤
4. My colleagues think I have a good sense of humor.	①	②	③	④	⑤
5. Good leaders have strong convictions.	①	②	③	④	⑤
6. I regard compassion as essential to my ability to lead others.	①	②	③	④	⑤

1 — Strongly Disagree 2 — Disagree 3 — Neutral
4 — Agree 5 — Strongly Agree

Rate Yourself

If you scored between…

26–30 Excellent leadership skills
25–20 Good leadership abilities
19–15 Learning to lead
>15 Need improvement

Action Planner: Understanding Your Character.

The foundation of effective leadership is character. While character is something that we accrue over time based upon our life experiences, it is possible to emphasize our strong features and learn to downplay our weaknesses. For example, if you are the kind of person who naturally likes people, you can learn to use that trait in your dealings with people who report to you. By contrast, if you are the kind of person who is quick to anger, you can learn techniques that may help you defuse your "hot-button" and to assess situations more calmly and rationally. Use this action planner as your guide to understanding your character better.

Reflective Questions

1. Make an inventory of your character traits. Once you have completed the exercise, ask yourself:

   • What are my strong traits? Consider them as your effective leadership traits.

   • How are those effective leadership traits useful in leadership situations?

   • How may those traits be harmful in leadership situations?

   • What are my weaknesses? Consider them as your ineffective leadership traits.

   • How might those ineffective leadership traits affect my willingness to lead?

2. Share the inventory of your effective and ineffective leadership traits and the mind-map with a trusted colleague. Solicit their opinion of your self-assessment.

3. Consider ways you can put your effective character traits to use

   • At work (Apply a willingness to listen to a colleague who is having trouble with a specific job assignment.)

   • At home (Apply your sense of patience to your spouse and children, or others you live with.)

4. Consider ways you can minimize your ineffective character traits

   • At work (Make a conscious effort to acknowledge the contributions of others.)

   • At home (Be creative in the way you communicate with your family or others around you.)

5. One of the challenges of leadership character is integrating the personal, professional, and social aspects of your life. Ideally, we want to create harmony between all parts of ourselves. To help you get a better sense of yourself, draw a mind map (or pictogram) of your personal commitments, responsibilities and passions. As you draw, consider how you can integrate all of them holistically. [This drawing depicts different elements of life, private and public that come together in one individual. Your drawing may be similar, or completely different. After all, no two people are exactly alike.]

Developing the Whole Leadership Character

> *The world of tomorrow belongs to the person*
> *who has the vision today.*
>
> REV. ROBERT SCHULLER

CHAPTER 3

Creating a Leadership Vision

When John F. Kennedy issued the challenge in May of 1961 to send a man to the moon and bring him back safely by the end of the decade, he set forth a clear vision of what he wanted NASA to accomplish. In retrospect, it does not matter that the challenge was born of Cold War politics and was meant more for external consumption—i.e., a challenge to the Soviet Union. NASA management and engineers rallied to the cause and made the trip to the moon a reality. Kennedy's proclamation was vision in its purest form. Likewise, we can look at the Declaration of Independence as an example of exceptional leadership vision. It tapped into the hearts and minds of the people who wanted life, liberty, and pursuit of happiness and as a result a new nation emerged, one that endeavored to make the vision real.

Every organization needs to have a clear, focused vision of the future. Leaders are initially responsible for creating that vision, or look into the future. If you examine successful companies, it is easy to discern which have a sharp sense of where they are headed. Cisco Systems, General Electric and Wal-Mart probably top everyone's list as examples of highly-focused companies.

Every successful enterprise results from a sharp vision. Focus: Hope, a nonprofit social service organization in Detroit, is very direct in its vision as evidenced by its mission statement which says in part, "to build a metropolitan community where all people may live in freedom, harmony, trust, and affection." [1] Toward that end, everyone at Focus: Hope understands what it takes to implement that vision and actively strives to achieve it every day. Employees and volunteers are united in the cause of social justice and equal opportunity for all. The visions of NASA, our Founding Fathers, and Focus: Hope are clear, concise, and focused. They also are vivid examples of leadership vision at work. [Note: Focus: Hope is described more fully in the chapter on Eleanor Josaitis.]

Leadership Vision Model

Leadership above all provides a sense of guidance, somewhere for others to follow. It is imperative that the leaders use their vision to express where they are going and why. So what are the key components of an effective vision that you can implement in your leadership?

Personal Vision

Focus on Goals

Tap into Aspirations

Adapt to Change

Share with Others

Lead to Inspiration

Leadership Vision

Leadership Vision Model

Focus on Goals

In their book, *Leaders*, eminent leadership consultants Warren Bennis and Burt Nanus state, "Management of attention through vision is the creating of focus....[Leaders'] visions are compelling and they pull people toward them."[2] Coaches often speak of the need for focusing on goals: why? When a team is focused—i.e., everyone understands the "big picture"—playing the game becomes the priority. Players can focus on what they do best without worrying about what fellow players are doing because they know everyone is doing his job. The same holds for business. A leader must communicate corporate and team goals with her people prior to making job assignments, so everyone can do the job with an understanding of where the department is headed. [Not everyone may agree with the goals, but at least everyone is aware of them.]

Tap into Aspirations

Effective leaders have the ability to relate their goals to the inner ambitions of their followers. History, of course, has been witness to the excesses where the leader infuses his warped vision with the baser instincts of his followers; Nazism and Stalinism are two notable tragedies.

Fortunately, there are many more examples of leaders drawing inspiration for their visions from the aspirations of their people. Theodore Roosevelt's leadership skills echoed the pride and emerging nationalist spirit of turn-of-the-20th-century America as he led the U.S. internationally against foreign infringement in our hemisphere. And domestically, his crusading spirit against monopolies echoed the hopes of the common man versus the robber barons.

Leaders do well to capture the spirit of their people. Management philosopher Peter Drucker, frames aspiration very well in his classic study, *The Practice of Management,* with the parable of the stonecutter:

"An old story tells of three stone cutters who were asked what they were doing. The first replied, 'I am making a living.' The second kept on hammering while he said, 'I am doing the best job of stonecutting in the entire country.' The third one looked up with a visionary gleam in his eyes, and said, 'I am building a cathedral.'"[3]

Leaders want to tap into what the third stone cutter is doing—the willingness to dream and work to build another future.

Adapt to Change

As crucial as the need for a vision to provide direction is, it must also flex with the reality of change. Since change is endemic to daily life, we must constantly adapt the vision to changing circumstances.

In many ways the concept of vision and the dynamics of change butt heads: vision points toward the future, the change throws roadblocks into the path of the future. Yet the two concepts need not be diametrically opposed. Successful visions are those that flex with time and bend with the will of the people. Our Founding Fathers knew this when they created the Bill of Rights as the first ten amendments to the Constitution. Many more amendments have been added over the past 200 years and no doubt more will be added in the future to adapt to society's evolving needs. [Note: We will explore the concept of leading change in Chapter 9.]

Share with Others

Vision sprung from the intellect of a few is a vision that likely will remain stuck on a few. One of the essential elements of a learning organization, as articulated by organizational learning architect Peter Senge, is the concept of the "shared vision."[4] While treatises have been written about what it takes to create shared vision, the essential truth is that a shared vision is one that others feel they can adapt and amend to meet individual and team needs. Ideally the vision stems from collaborative effort that, in turn, is embellished with the participation of everyone within the organization.

Does this mean everyone has to pen words to the corporate vision statement? No, that would be folly, as well as a collective waste of time. As a leader, you need to make the vision relevant and meaningful so that everyone feels a part of executing it in his daily routines. This is part of what it takes to make people feel involved and committed.

Lead Others to Inspiration

Vision serves as a compass to the future, but it can be more than a simple instrument. Vision ideally should generate the sense of possibility. Visions, as opposed to strategy statements, which articulate the means of achievement, simply set forth the goal. The famed retailer Nordstrom does it better than most; its employee handbook contains a single rule: "Use your good judgment in all situations." That statement does not delineate specific behaviors; it describes a philosophy toward life. Using "good judgment" trusts the employee to do what is right for the customer as well as for the business. As a result, employees feel inspired and personally committed to the Nordstrom vision.[5]

The Nordstrom vision is the kind that enables its employees to share in the execution as they expand their own horizons. And ultimately we want to unlock the potential of our people to enable them to achieve individual goals for themselves that mirror collective goals for the organization. By doing so, the organization and the people in it grow together.

Leadership Vision

Leadership based upon vision is fundamental to the success of an organization. It provides the purpose, clarity, and inspiration to rally people to the cause.

At the same time, vision cannot be imposed. It should be shared as discussed earlier, but it also can be allowed to evolve over time. In fact, visions should change. Leaders must allow, even encourage, alternative thinking regarding vision-process. Just as you change your outlook, so too, must visions. What was right for a company in 1980 may not be right in the year 2000. Arie de Geus in his book, *Living Company*, discusses the evolution of a 700-year old company that began as a mining operation. Today, the Swedish company, Stora, is a paper pulp and chemical company. Stora successfully adapted to seven centuries worth of change. And it is still changing.[6]

Likewise, visions, like people who create them, should evolve. If the principles remain rooted in personal growth and employee participation, the vision may evolve, but it will not reverse itself. It will simply focus on new challenges as they arise.

The lesson, therefore, is not to spend so much time on vision that it becomes the stuff of lore. Such an approach would defeat the original intent: to provide purpose and direction. Just as Thomas Jefferson worried about the excessive power of federalism and urged a continual state of renewal, so too, must leaders invest their energies in crafting a vision that is clear and direct, but also organic and capable of growth.

Ultimately, successful organizational visions build upon the core strengths of their people, leaders and followers alike. While some visions may emerge from the strong personal convictions of the leader who rallies others to the power of the cause, their success requires that leaders and followers work together to fulfill the mission of the organization.

Self-Assessment: Building a Personal Vision

Vision is essential to personal growth as well as leadership of others. Use this assessment to see how you rate your own leadership vision.

Leadership Vision Assessment					
1. I am focused on my goals and do not waver in my commitment to them.	①	②	③	④	⑤
2. Shared vision is important to leading others.	①	②	③	④	⑤
3. I view change as an opportunity for personal growth.	①	②	③	④	⑤
4. Leadership requires an ability to persuade others to follow.	①	②	③	④	⑤
5. I believe it is important to share credit with others.	①	②	③	④	⑤
6. Leadership vision must adapt to change, otherwise it is doomed to fail.	①	②	③	④	⑤

1 — Strongly Disagree   2 — Disagree   3 — Neutral
4 — Agree   5 — Strongly Agree

Rate Yourself

If you scored between...

26–30 Excellent leadership skills
25–20 Good leadership abilities
19–15 Learning to lead
 >15 Need improvement

Action Planner: Creating a Strong Personal Vision

Leaders must know from where they have been and where they are going. Vision serves as the lodestone for leadership. It points leaders in the right direction. This Action Planner will help you discover more about your own vision, and help you refine your outlook for leadership.

Reflective Questions

1. Make an inventory of your past work experience. Once you have completed the exercise, ask yourself:

   • What job experience helped me the most? Why?

   • What can you take from that positive experience that will make you a better leader?

   • What job experience hurt me the most? Why?

   • What can you use from that negative experience to make you a better leader?

2. What character in history do you admire most? Why?

3. What character from your personal life (work, school, family) do you admire most? Why?

4. Where do you want to be in five years?

- At work

- At home

5. Where do you want to be in one year?

- At work

- At home

6. Think of yourself as a business. Create a personal mission statement for that "business." Use the following questions to shape your statement. Try to keep your mission statement under 100 words.

- What do you do? (Manager, engineer, lawyer, etc.)

- Whom do you serve? (Who is your customer?)

- What do you offer? (What service to you offer?)

- What is your commitment? (How do you want to serve your customer: promptly, efficiently, cost-effectively, etc.)

7. Using your mission statement, write a job description for your ideal job.

8. Write a short obituary for yourself. Highlight the contributions that you would like others to remember about you.

9. List those attributes for which you would like to be remembered. If they are behaviors, practice them daily. If they are aspirations, think of ways to make them come true.

> *Strategy is not the consequence of planning,*
> *but the opposite: its starting point.*
>
> HENRY MINTZBERG

CHAPTER 4

Developing a Leadership Strategy

Strategy is one of those business topics that seem to go in and out of favor. During the Post-World War II boom, strategy was in full favor. The goal in those days was to meet production to fulfill an insatiable consumer demand for goods. For many companies, it was simply a matter of keeping production high enough to meet volume. Strategy was more an effort of planning: sourcing raw materials, keeping the factory operating, and shipping orders. Predictability dictated strategy.

When America's boom waned, the need for strategy as it was then practiced was no longer necessary. Instead of a production economy, we moved to a full-market economy where the source of power shifted from production to consumer. The consumer dictated corporate moves. Unpredictability was the watchword. With this sea change, the need for strategy—as a form of forward planning—was seen by many to be unnecessary.

This change did not negate the need for strategy, it simply ended the need for strategy as it had been practiced previously. In today's global economy, filled with a myriad of trends and counter trends, the need for strategy has never been greater. It is this element of unpredictability that makes it so necessary to think ahead. Some may be tempted to think that if you can't predict anything, don't worry and just let things happen as they may. In some matters, such as love and courtship, this approach may be appropriate. But this laissez-faire attitude would be disastrous for business.

Imagine yourself running a small business, say a sandwich shop. Would you simply rent space, buy kitchen equipment, outfit the interior, procure your supplies without first doing some initial research? Not likely. For example, you would determine what businesses are located nearby your site; what employees of those businesses do during their lunch break; what food choices these employees have; and finally, who else is servicing sandwiches. The results of your research will form the basis for a strategy for entering the sandwich business or choosing some other line of work.

Leaders need to know how they will reach their goals. Strategy provides leaders with the "how-to" of achievement. A business leader who wants to grow his business must consider a host of strategic factors, including the competitiveness of the product line, the ability to service the products, the skills of the management team, and the abilities of his work force. For each of these factors, the leader and her managers must devise strategies that will capitalize on their strong points and eliminate their weak points. These strategies will likely involve capital improvements to manufacturing facilities as well as investments in training to improve the skills of their employees. Each of the steps the team utilizes to accomplish their aims are strategies.

Just as organizations need strategies to enable them to achieve their goals, so do people. You as a leader need to have a personal strategy that shows you and your people the best way to achieve your vision and your goals.

What Are the Fundamentals of Personal Strategy?

Vision: Knowing Where You Want to Go

Vision, as we discussed in the last chapter, is fundamental to leadership because it forms your end goal. For example, a biology student in college may wish to be a doctor. That's his vision. Likewise, a young woman beginning as a copywriter in an advertising agency may aspire to be creative director. Again, that's a vision.

Objectives: What You Want to Do When You Get There

Vision is essential to leadership, but just as a traveler might know his destination, it is wise to know what you wish to do when you arrive. For example, the young man who wants to be a doctor must formulate objectives. What kind of physician does he want to be? A family practitioner, or an orthopedic surgeon. What kind of a practice does he want to belong to? A small team or a part of a hospital group.

Likewise, the aspiring creative director should begin to think about what kind of advertising she would like to create. Is she going for cutting-edge themes, or traditional, heart-warming values? What kind of a pace does she intend to set? How will she work with other members of the creative team?

The answers to these questions lead to the formation of objectives.

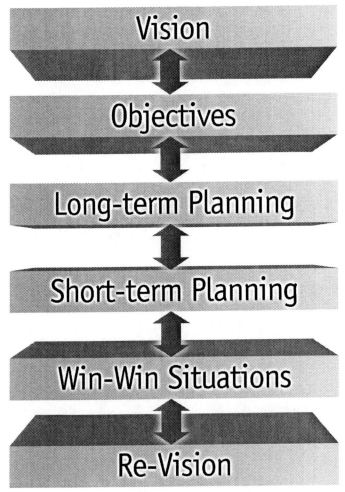

Vision

Objectives

Long-term Planning

Short-term Planning

Win-Win Situations

Re-Vision

Personal Leadership Strategy Model

Long-Term Plans: Finding Ways to Get There Over Time

Knowing where you want to go and what you want to do when you arrive is not the end. You have to determine the right path. For the future medical student, he must continue his education and strive for high marks. For the future creative director, she must continue to produce good, strong copy that achieves recognition.

Both of the young people should find ways to continue their education. For the pre-med student the choice is obvious: stay in school. For the creative director in waiting, maybe taking additional courses at an art school or continuing education through seminars is effective.

Networking (which we will discuss momentarily) also is important. It is important to find role models. You can either do this from afar; i.e., the look and learn approach. Or you can do it up close, get to know the person on an individual basis. If the role model is willing to be a mentor, that is a big bonus.

Short-Term Plans: Finding Ways to Get There Now

Getting there right away is not a fantasy. It can be closer than you think. For example, the pre-med student may find summer internships in science or research. The creative director may seek more challenging job assignments. Short-term planning can be an effective way to gain valuable knowledge that will help the attainment of the short-term goal.

Win-Win Situations: Give Yourself a Chance to Celebrate

Becoming a doctor is a long quest. It does not occur overnight. It takes discipline over years. Yet the student needs affirmation that he is on the right path. Good grades are strong affirmations of success. So too are letters of reference from professors and employers.

Likewise, creative directors are not born; they are developed. Our young lady must learn to view each creative assignment as a possibility of doing excellent work. When the ads gain recognition from peers and awards from professional associations, the copywriter will know that she is on the correct path.

We call these affirmations "win-win" situations. They are essential to achievement; consider them as milestone events. Celebrate them. The pride you derive from overcoming challenges or registering achievements will fuel your long climb to achieve your vision.

Re-Vision: Prepare Yourself to Do It Again

Knowing where you want to go is essential to leadership, but so too is the realization that the vision may change after you arrive, or before you get there.

Changing direction, either in a big or small way, takes courage. For example, if our young pre-med student does not have the grades for medical school, he should begin to consider an alternative career, either in nursing, medical technology, or some other field entirely. This change does not mean failure; it means confronting reality. Likewise, if our creative director achieves her goal, she may discover that it is not what she wants after all. Perhaps the job is less artistic than anticipated—a management position that takes time way from creative development.

Having the sense to alter a vision—as well as the strategies involved to achieve it—requires soul-searching and the strength of conviction. It is not a process that should be undertaken alone. Confer with colleagues, friends, and family—whomever you trust. Keep in mind that life is a continual process of change. Just because you have a vision at the outset of your career does not mean you must—or should—fulfill it. Personal leadership provides you with the inner sense of direction you need to decide.

These examples primarily concern young people. But developing a personal strategy is not an exercise confined to youth. All of us—at any stage in our lives—need to know where we are headed, how we will get there, what we will do when we arrive, and how we will continue to keep our vision fresh. Personal leadership demands a measure of continuous personal assessment.

Act Like a Leader

If you are to accomplish your vision and goals, you must exert personal leadership; i.e., the will to make things happen. So think like a leader! Ask yourself the same questions that shaped your vision and plans.

- Where I am going?
- How will I get there?
- How will my decisions affect me and my people?
- The answers to these questions will form the basis of your leadership strategies.

Maintain Alignment of Vision, Strategy, and Objectives

Alignment is essential to strategies. Your strategies and your objectives should always been in alignment with your vision. On a personal level, you want to keep yourself pointed toward your goals, that is, aligned with your personal vision. On an organizational level, you want every departmental vision to be consistent with the overall organizational vision. Alignment of departmental and corporate objectives is paramount. Otherwise, the organization loses focus if everyone is doing his own thing.

Alignment, however, should not preclude creativity. It is essential that leaders encourage freedom of thought and action. The challenge is to keep that creativity consistent with corporate directives. For example, manufacturing operations can encourage their engineers to think of new ways to streamline processes, to make things simpler and easier. Such an objective is in alignment with the corporate goals of reducing costs and improving customer satisfaction.

Value of Networking Strategically

As part of your personal leadership strategy, you should find ways to network with other leaders in other organizations. By talking to them you will find that many of them are just like you, facing similar challenges about life and work. Your conversations may lead you to discover some valuable insights that you may apply to your own situation.

To network successfully, you need to be strategic. Look to network where you think you can learn the most. You may start by networking with individuals from your current job. Consider joining a professional or trade organizations; such organizations are designed to enable members to interact and learn from one another. You also may network with people from your community, church, or volunteer organization. Shared experience is a strong basis for networking because it forms a common bond upon which you can build a relationship.

Networking is, by nature, a two-way street. Just as you learn from others, make certain that others are learning from you. If you think of networking as merely "taking," you will get something, but if you take a strategic view, and think of networking as "taking and receiving," you will ultimately learn much more.

Personal Leadership Strategy

Strategy, as mentioned at the outset of this chapter, is a concept that seems to come in and out of favor. Exerting a personal leadership strategy, however, will always be important. It is essential to your personal development as a leader as well as your ability to provide clear direction for your organization.

Self-Assessment: Creating a Leadership Strategy

Having a leadership strategy is essential to developing plans and fulfilling objectives. Use this assessment to measure your ability to develop a personal strategy.

Leadership Strategy Assessment					
1. I have a plan to implement my vision for my life.	①	②	③	④	⑤
2. I believe it is important to let people know where we are headed.	①	②	③	④	⑤
3. I view strategy as a bridge to tomorrow.	①	②	③	④	⑤
4. The capacity to learn and grow depends upon having an effective plan.	①	②	③	④	⑤
5. I have taken what I learned in one job (school) and applied it to future jobs.	①	②	③	④	⑤
6. Networking strategically; i.e., choosing people who can help you learn—can be beneficial to personal growth.	①	②	③	④	⑤

1—Strongly Disagree   2—Disagree   3—Neutral
4—Agree   5—Strongly Agree

Rate Yourself

If you scored between...

26–30 Excellent leadership skills
25–20 Good leadership abilities
19–15 Learning to lead
 >15 Need improvement

Action Planner: Building a Leadership Strategy

If vision points you in the right direction, strategy shows you how to get there. This Action Planner will provide you with ideas to help you plan and implement your long and short-term strategies.

Reflective Questions

1. Read your mission statement and job description. Think about how you will make it happen in the long-term

   • Need to change careers?

   • Need more schooling?

   • Need a mentor?

2. Referring to your mission statement and job description, think about how you will make it happen in the short-term?

   • Need to change jobs?

   • Need to take course?

   • Need to network?

   • Need a source of supplemental income to enable yourself to accomplish your goals?

3. In the text we described acting like a leader. Here's an exercise you can do to assess your leadership skills.

Assume for a moment you are an inventor who has just developed a new invention. One large company likes your invention so much they want to buy it for one million dollars. By selling it, you assign all ownership rights to the company. A group of venture capitalists also likes your concept and is willing to provide you funding to start a business around your new invention. You are not a businessperson, but you have a trusted friend who is. She is willing to partner with you and take a 25% equity stake in the new business. The venture capitalists could take another 25% equity stake in the business, leaving you with total ownership of the invention and a 50% stake in the new business.

What will you do?

To answer it, think strategically—long term and short term. (There are no right or wrong answers; this is an exercise to develop your skills.)

- How important is money to me?

- Do I want to ensure ownership of my invention?

- If I took the money for my invention, what would I do next?

- Do I want to go into business with a friend?

- Do I want to build a business where there are no guarantees?

4. Apply these same questions to your work situation today. Before you answer, take a moment to reflect on the consequences.

- Will I continue in my present position?

- Do I need to get further formal education? (i.e., M.B.A., M.S. in Engineering, etc.)

- How will my decisions affect my future career aspirations?

- What will my career advancement mean for my family?

- Do I value environment in which I work today?

> *Time is the scarcest resource, and unless it is managed nothing else can be managed.*
>
> PETER DRUCKER

CHAPTER 5

Maximizing Time to Lead

There are certainly many theories concerning leadership as well as many descriptions of its attributes, but I would surmise that most people would agree that leaders have one thing in common: not enough time. That is unfortunate because effective leadership requires time: to think, to plan, to manage, and above all, to serve the needs of the people.

But despite our best intentions, we are faced with serious time constraints. Here are two big reasons why.

First, leaders require time to proclaim their message and followers need time to respond. Genuine leadership requires commitment that may not always occur overnight. Leaders who counsel urgency often confront the fact that time is running out and the need to act quickly and efficiently is upon them. Entrepreneurs and newly appointed corporate leaders often feel overwhelmed by the enormity of the task that confronts them. Imagine the challenge of starting a new business, hiring a team of people, refining the product or service, finding the right markets, promoting and distributing it. The list goes on. Naturally, under these circumstances, leaders may feel that they do not have enough time to accomplish all of their tasks.

Second, some leaders fall into the trap of letting the job get the better of their supervisory time. The details can accumulate from every source: excess paperwork, voluminous email, too many meetings, intrusions from subordinates, and meddling from superiors. The net result is that leaders spend more time managing details rather than fulfilling the parameters of a job. When this occurs, the details of the job outweigh the value of the job itself.

Leaders who do not manage their time effectively, begin to find their organizations and even themselves spiral slowly out of control. When it happens, leadership goes out the window and chaos reigns in its place.

Managing your time effectively is not easy. The pressure to get things done dictates our daily lives, even on vacation. According to a survey sponsored by AT&T, nearly half of all employees take cell phones along on trips in order to stay in touch with the office.[1] And if you own your own business you may never feel you can take a vacation at all.

It's at times like this we ask: are we managing our jobs, or are they managing us?

Our lives are a jumble of *got-to's*—big assignments that must be completed.

- *Got to* meet business objectives.
- *Got to* keep the boss in the loop.
- *Got to* meet personal performance objectives.
- *Got to* finish the major project, along with all the little ones along the way.

To this list of *got to's,* you can add a slew of *should's*—little things that need constant attention.

- *Should* complete the paperwork.
- *Should* return phone messages.
- *Should* keep current on e-mail.
- *Should* keep people informed.

Between the *got to's* and the *should's,* where is the "time for you to lead"?

Too often, the sheer volume of the workload—things you have to get done—coupled with speed—deadlines you have to meet—collide head-on. We are left to reel dazedly from one task to another, never really sure of our next step. No one in this state can lead an organization, let alone himself.

Time Management Guidelines

Here are some suggestions for successful time management that will help you restore balance to your life and enable you to lead more effectively.

Set Priorities

Determine what is important to you personally and professionally. Make a distinction between long-term and short-term goals. For example, if you are determined to complete an assignment, do it with distinction. Focus on the task at hand and minimize distractions. On the other hand,

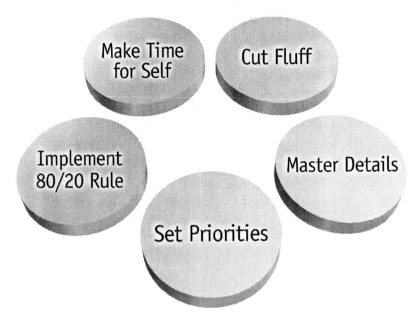

Time Management Diagram

if you are interested in advancing in your career, choose a position or a job that you would like to have. Look at those who are currently holding that position and set about acquiring their skills and background. It may mean going back to school or changing jobs to do it.

On the personal front, family life is a priority. The common gripe is: "I don't have enough time." The comeback line is: "Make time for it." Mothers and fathers can become involved in their children's school as teacher assistants, or on the playing fields as coaches. The point is if you want to do it, you can do it. One day a week come home at five, or spend a lunch hour at school instead of at work. The rewards you will receive from being with your children will outweigh anything you do at work.

Over and above these activities, set time aside during the week or weekend. Make no other commitments. At the same time, be realistic with yourself; there are times when job demands can be excessively time consuming. If you are involved in a time-consuming project at work, make a promise to yourself that you will make extra time for the family when the project is over. This bargain with yourself will allow you to complete the project with the knowledge that you can and do have a family, and will make time for them.

Implement 80/20 Rule

At the turn of the 20th century, an Italian economist Vilfredo Pareto posited an interesting metric: 80% of wealth was derived from 20% of economic assets. Today we can apply the same principle to the management of our time by concentrating the bulk of your time on your most important projects or relationships. That is, devote 80% of your time to the top 20% of your priorities.

Do not become distracted with little side details that can detract from your most important relationships. At the same time you must be aware that change will occur and what is of little importance today may be significantly important tomorrow. For example, a marketing manager responsible for a mainstay product and a couple of new products may concentrate on the power-hitter, but understand that in time, one of the new products may take off.

The same principle applies to family life. A couple with no children can have a great deal of time for one another. Once children appear, their "alone" time will be reduced, or even disappear. Yet, over time, the commitment to each other should remain and they can, and will if they want to, renew their relationship in other ways.

Master the Details

Don't let them master you. Modern work life seems like a jumble of details. And the outlook does not appear much brighter. While we have become much more adept at receiving and managing information, the human brain has not increased its ability to process it more efficiently. The lesson is to create ways to prioritize details and attend only to the important things. Ignore the rest. Here are some suggestions:

- *Scan memos.* Read and file important ones, discard the rest.
- *Skim email.* Scan the headings. Open and read the ones that pertain to you. Trash the rest.
- *Strive to reduce number of meetings.* Not every decision requires a meeting. Important decisions may require input, but decisions about minor details can be handled more efficiently in one-to-one sessions.
- *Delegate details to others.* Do not shift the burden, shift responsibility. Empower your people to handle things. If your subordinates are overburdened, encourage them to concentrate on the important things.

- *Starve the beast.* Some organizations fall into the trap of performing work that does not add value to the enterprise. People work only to "feed the beast"—e.g., the organization. A case in point might be an engineering firm that requires approval for every step in the design. After awhile, the engineers are seeking approval from one another without adding value to the process or the customer. Eliminate the hierarchy, and the requisite number of sign-offs, and the work will be accomplished more efficiently. By "starving the beast," managers free time for their employees to think creatively, formulate new ideas, and implement new solutions. All of these activities add value to work.

Cut the Fluff

By examining your priorities, you can find time for what really matters. Elaine St. James was a successful real estate broker with properties in Connecticut and Southern California. Her success inspired her to write a book and take to the lecture circuit. But while her business was booming, she felt she was neglecting her personal life. So St. James began to scale back. She turned her writing talents to creating a series of books that concentrate on maintaining a simple way of life. Among the techniques St. James advocates are:[2]

- *Make time for what you enjoy doing in work and in play.* It may be obvious that many people do not like the work they do, but people have always done things for money. What is distressing is the fact many people do not enjoy their leisure time.[3] When you like your work, you will do it better because work ceases to be a drudgery, it becomes pleasurable. Likewise when you are not working, you are entitled to some enjoyment. Relaxation is essential to the human spirit, so when it comes to leisure time, find an activity you enjoy doing and do it. If you tire of it, forget it. And therein lies the difference between work and play. You cannot always quit an unpleasant job, but you should always be able to abandon a leisure activity that ceases to be fun.

- *Live by the "less is more" creed.* Live on less than your entire income and save what's left over. (Easier said than done, but you get the picture). Acting to limit spending frees you from having to work in order to pay for possessions. (And think of all the time you will save by not shopping.)

- *Do not commit yourself to too many different things.* Modern life has become a compromise between what "is important" and what "seems important." In other words, everything may seem like a "got-to" but it may not really be so. By saying no to certain perceived obligations you may free yourself up to do what you really need to do. This attitude is not selfishness per se; it's self-preservation. And I would argue that by freeing your time you can do more with and for your family as well as in your community.

- *Limit your possessions.* Too much stuff cannot only clutter your work and living spaces, they can clog up your lifestyle. In other words, don't buy it unless you truly need and use it.

- *Concentrate on what is essential to you personally and professionally.* At work, focus on tasks that satisfy customers and increase shareholder value. At home, focus on putting the needs of spouse and children first. In this way, you will increase your own contribution to family values.

Make Time for Yourself

Leaders need time for themselves. "Put down a list of the 20 things you're doing that make you work 90 hours," says Jack Welch, CEO of General Electric, "and 10 of them have to be nonsense, or somebody else has got to do them for you." [4] [Incidentally, Welch is a terrific golfer with a 3.8 handicap index according to a *Golf Digest* rating of June, 1998.]

Adequate time affords the leader the opportunity to examine what is going on around him. The leader can use this self-examination to reflect on his progress. From this examination, the leader may find new solutions to old problems. Sometimes the simple act of stepping back and looking at the problem in a new light can generate solutions. [Chapter10 will deal with the topic of reflection.]

Time as a Resource

Time management is an essential leadership behavior. Thinking of time as a resource may be your most valuable asset as a leader. Without enough time, a leader will seem like a spinning dervish wildly giving orders that no one will hear, let alone do. With enough time, the leader can create an opportunity for people and their ideas to come together in a creative mixture that can over weeks, months, and years propel the organization to the next level of improved performance.

Self-Assessment: Managing Your Time

Time is, of course, your most precious resource. Personal leadership demands that you use it wisely. Use this assessment to see how you are managing your time now.

Leadership Time Management Assessment					
1. I regard time as a resource that I must invest wisely.	①	②	③	④	⑤
2. It is not necessary to finish each and every task; sometimes it is necessary for others to finish the assignment.	①	②	③	④	⑤
3. Delegating responsibility may be the first lesson of effective time management.	①	②	③	④	⑤
4. My people think that I encourage them to use their time wisely.	①	②	③	④	⑤
5. If I feel my company is not putting our people's time to good use, I will speak out.	①	②	③	④	⑤
6. Reflection requires taking time away from the job to assess how I am doing.	①	②	③	④	⑤

1 — Strongly Disagree   2 — Disagree   3 — Neutral
4 — Agree   5 — Strongly Agree

Rate Yourself

If you scored between…

26–30 Excellent leadership skills
25–20 Good leadership abilities
19–15 Learning to lead
 >15 Need improvement

Action Planner: Managing Your Time

Time management is a matter of personal responsibility. You cannot do everything you need to do in a day, so you must learn habits and strategies that enable you to take control of what you do. This Action Planner will help you list your time commitments and find ways to manage them more effectively. The net result will be a gain in time that you can use to lead more effectively.

Reflective Questions

1. Create a list of your daily work activities. Assign a percentage of time you spend on each.

2. Isolate your least important category. Consider ways you can reduce time in this activity.

3. Isolate your most important category. Ask yourself if you are spending enough time doing it. Consider ways you can invest more time in this activity.

4. Create a list of your family activities. Assign a percentage of time you spend on each.

5. Make a list of your priorities. Include work and family. Assign a percentage of time you spend on each.

6. Examine your list. Ask yourself what can you do to maximize time spent on your priorities.

7. Make a schedule of your daily activities. Fill in the hours.

Work

7:00	1:00
8:00	2:00
9:00	3:00
10:00	4:00
11:00	5:00
12:00	6:00

After Work

7:00	9:00
8:00	10:00

8. Once you have filled in the schedule look at those activities under the following criteria:

   • List activities that require more time.

   • List activities that require less time.

   • List activities that can be eliminated.

   • Make a new schedule.

9. What can you do to free up time for reflection; e.g., thinking about issues and your role in them?

It takes two to speak the truth—
one to speak and one to hear.

HENRY DAVID THOREAU

CHAPTER 6

Communicating Leadership

Effective communications is words and thoughts in action.

People who study communications like to use the term "active listening." Active listening is engaged listening; it involves receiving the message, analyzing it, then responding. It involves body language, maintaining a posture that is open, rather than closed.

By extension, the precursor to active listening is "active speaking." Active speakers, like active listeners, maintain eye contact and engage their body physically with their words. Most important, active speakers strive for clear, concise communication. Directness is a virtue; mixed messages are vices. In normal conversation, active speaking and listening is like a tennis match. Serve with words, volley with facial expressions, and rally with words and behaviors. It is natural.

Active speaking and listening will deliver dividends in the form of employees who feel they can communicate to you as well as to colleagues. As the leader, you set the tone for the team. More importantly, listening indicates that you care. When listeners perceive genuine concern, it opens the door to communication that is honest and enduring.

Leading Aloud: Active Speaking

How well you lead depends upon how well you speak. The ability to communicate an idea—as grandiose as a vision, or as humble as a change to a speech—depends upon the ability to think clearly and to articulate those thoughts precisely and concisely. The very fundamentals of leadership communication depend upon the leader's ability to express herself in ways that leave no doubt as to intent, meaning, and direction.

Good leaders do it instinctively. During the 1992 Presidential campaign, the American public was treated to a display of "out loud leadership." Whereas President George Bush waffled and used run-on sentences that sounded like a cross between a policy briefing and a poorly written high school term paper, Clinton's words were simple, direct, and on point.

The rules of communications that politicians follow (or don't follow) are the same as for business leaders. When a CEO stands up before a group of securities analysts to declare that his company will achieve a ten percent gain in earnings, he is definite and direct. When he speaks in front of his managers, he must be equally assured in articulating how the company will achieve those aims: cut costs, improve efficiencies, and raise quality. Clear, concise, and to the point. No waffling, no hesitation.

Here are some points that manager-leaders can use to keep their words and actions aligned with their vision and strategies.

Model for Active Speaking

Think Ahead

Think before you open your mouth. It is something your mother probably taught you and your elementary school teachers reminded you to do. For leaders, thought should always precede words and actions.

Gayle Cohen of Well-Spoken, Inc., a much-in-demand executive speech coaching firm, emphasizes two important points to her clients:

reason and purpose. "Know the reason you are on stage and communicate the purpose of why you are there."

Public relations professionals advise their clients to formulate answers to specific questions before meeting with the media. This practice could apply to leaders in any situation. Think of how you will articulate a plan to your people before you present it. Anticipate their reaction and formulate responses. Come up with possible responses. Let the answers play over and over in your mind before saying them aloud. The important point is to think ahead; don't just "wing it."

Be Clear and Consistent

First and foremost, make your message clear—that is, easily understood. Second, ensure that your message is consistent—in keeping with what you said before. If you mentally outline your thoughts, you will speak more clearly. Consistency is important because it concerns character. A leader who continually flip-flops lacks decisiveness. "Be clear with what you want to do with the audience: persuade, sell, inspire, or reassure," says Cohen. "When you are certain in your purpose, the more effective you will be as a speaker."

At the same time, consistency does permit a leader to change his mind. When this occurs, however, the leader must define the exact reasons why he is changing his opinion. Such a change will then be consistent with a leader who is assured in his thinking and precise in his words and actions.

Practice Aloud

When I was in Catholic grammar school, the good sisters taught us that anyone who talked to himself was crazy. With respect to my childhood teachers, I beg to differ. It is important for leaders to say their thoughts aloud as a means of crystallizing their thinking. Not to verbalize internally is what's crazy. Saying ideas aloud (even in whispers) focuses the mind on arranging words in a neat, logical order. Practicing aloud for a speech appearance, alone or with a trusted associate, is mandatory. The mind and tongue need to work together; practice makes perfect.

Engage Physically

Just as communications involves more than words, so too, does presentation. As a speech coach, Cohen reminds us that how things are said matter sometimes more than the words themselves. "The vocal intonation and visual accompaniment of face and body underscore the message. If the voice is unsure, or the gestures forced, the audience will think that you do not believe what you are saying." That reaction, of course, is deadly and will kill a presentation, or sour a face-to-face meeting more quickly than words themselves.

Proper enunciation, correct pitch, and firm modulation are essential to projecting words. Effective body language is equally imperative. When you talk, your body should resonate with meaning. Uncross those arms. Don't slouch, or slur your words. Look directly at the person to whom you are speaking. Make eye contact and hold it. Engage your body in the conversation. Using your body to speak does not mean you must pretend to be Italian with plenty of hand gestures; it does mean, however, that your stance should be open and friendly and your gestures should be genuine. That reflects interest in the other person.

For more formal occasions, such as a speech, practice standing erect. The choice of using a podium for prepared remarks, or wandering the stage, is up to the presenter. Naturalism is in. Talk to the audience as you would a friend. Engage the audience in a conversation with your eyes, your gestures, and your vocalization.

Listen

Every leader needs to spend time listening. The more I reflect upon leadership, the more I place value on listening. Find out what the other person is thinking. See how your ideas play in the eyes of your listeners. If your words are not sparking interest, you are not communicating; you're simply droning.

At the same time, listening involves receiving information. Listen to what other people are saying about your ideas. Too much praise could mean they could care less; too much criticism could mean the same. Judge for yourself how your words resonate with your people. Leaders need also to tune their messages to the needs of their listeners. This is more than telling people what they want to hear. It means your remarks, formal and informal, need to reflect the concerns of your people.

Tell Stories

Just as one picture is worth a thousand words, one good anecdote may be worth ten thousand words. Some leaders approach public speaking from the viewpoint of "I want to tell you a story...." Their words and actions stem from an inner narrative that reflects their personality and colors everything they utter.

Even if a leader is not a natural storyteller, narratives are still appropriate. The stories may be anecdotal, apocryphal, or inspirational. Noel Tichy, leadership consultant and author, reminds us how Martin Luther King used stories to relate a vision of tomorrow. Roberto Goizueta used his company, Coca-Cola, and its people as a metaphor for communicating his message.[1]

In times of crisis, leaders might recall the serious: Winston Churchill rallying his people during the London Blitz of 1940; or less dramatically, Joe Namath predicting victory for his New York Jets over the seemingly invincible Baltimore Colts in 1969. Churchill was right. As was Namath.

Effective stories draw parallels between your situation and the situations of others. Abraham Lincoln was a master storyteller. He learned the skill from his father and later as a country lawyer traveling from town to town litigating case after case. Addressing different juries taught him how to relate the case to personal situations of the listeners. Although you do not want to change your core message for every audience, you do want to relate your ideas to everyday terms.

Keep in mind stories are not reserved for the stump. Good leaders use them in everyday conversation. President Lyndon Johnson was forever buttonholing people and regaling them with stories from his home state of Texas. His purpose was not strict entertainment; he was trying to persuade. And at that, Johnson was a master.

Apply Humor

Never take yourself too seriously. Humor is appropriate for nearly every occasion. It can be used to defuse a hostile audience, or win over a skeptical one. Here's another one from Lincoln. After the Battle of Bull Run, which saw the Union troops routed in the first major engagement of the Civil War, Lincoln's generals were trying to put some positive spin on the terrible defeat. Lincoln cut to the chase: "So, it is your notion that we whipped the rebels and then ran away from them?"[2]

Humor is best if it comes from deep within the speaker's own personality. It must be "organic" to her style and her sense of self. For this reason, many shy from humor; they may not know how to craft a joke or tell a funny story. Worse, they don't know how to deliver it convincingly. This situation is sad because laughter is an essential human emotion. Leaders can help themselves by learning to appreciate humor and using it appropriately.

Leadership Aloud and Aligned

All of the steps we have just reviewed will help you develop your leadership communications. But there is one more point you need to keep in mind: alignment. Align your communications—out loud and on paper—with corporate visions, strategies and objectives. In this way, you will keep everyone focused and in tune with the organization.

Speaking well and leading well go hand in hand. Leadership without effective communications is leadership without focus, direction, and ultimately followership.

Leadership by Ear: Active Listening

Speaking is only one half of communicating. The other half—or more—is listening.

The story goes that when legendary Hollywood director Cecil B. DeMille was making *The Ten Commandments,* he invested much time and resources to the scene where Moses parts the Red Sea. In an era before digital special effects, everything had to happen in real-time. The sequence involved complex and precise camera movement, expert blocking by actors and extras, and much behind-the-scenes maneuvering by grips and gaffers. Finally, DeMille called for the shot to begin; all went according to plan. The water dropped, the actors emoted, and the technology behaved. When all was over, the cameraman called out, "Ready when you are, Mr. DeMille." The entire scene had to be redone.

True? I cannot say for certain, but I do know that its message is true: not listening can have disastrous consequences. All of us are guilty of this from time to time. While we may not miss the parting of the Red Sea, we miss something greater—the opportunity to connect to our people in a meaningful and direct way.

Experts who study communications promote the virtues of "active listening." Active listening is engaged listening; it involves receiving the message, analyzing it, and then responding. Just like active speaking, active listening involves body language. Active listeners maintain an open posture and an expressive face.

Here are some techniques you may use to engage in active listening:

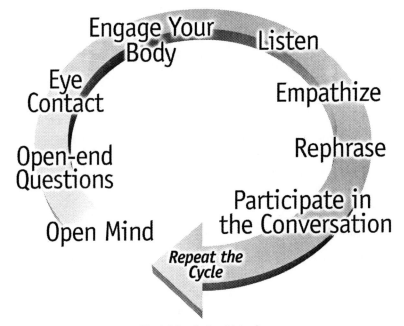

Model for Active Listening

- Approach with an open mind. (Don't pre-judge the situation.)
- Ask open-end questions (Those that begin with words like how, why, or tell me.)
- Maintain eye-contact (People want to see you.)
- Engage your body. (Uncross your arms, relax your muscles, and animate responses facially.)
- Listen to what the other person is saying. (Think before you reply.)
- Empathize with the situation. ("This reminds me of this situation that happened to me once…")
- Rephrase what the other person is saying. ("If I understand you correctly, you are saying…")
- Participate in the conversation. (Serve and volley; serve and volley.)
- Repeat the cycle until the entire session is concluded.

Some leaders believe that listening is the most vital element of communication because it opens the door to two-way communications between leader and follower. From that process both can develop an understanding of each other's needs. In his book *My American Journey,* General Colin Powell argues that a leader demonstrates concern by listening.[3]

For this reason active listening can be a good way to uncover work-place issues. By listening to what employees are saying and how they are saying it, you can learn what they are really thinking. For example, if employees are short with one another, including their boss, you can see that something is wrong. A manager confronting a situation like this has to approach carefully. Asking a blunt question such as "What's eating you?" will be regarded as a threat. A better approach calls for making small talk about non-work topics like family or sports. If you build a rapport over time, you can open the door to discuss more substantive issues regarding the work place. Furthermore, you will demonstrate what Colin Powell believes is an essential leadership attribute: concern for your followers.

Active Communications

Effective leadership communications demands individuals who are capable of speaking and listening—actively. It is not always easy to deliver the same message again and again, or listen patiently to subordinates tell you things you may already know, but these behaviors—along with all the others we have demonstrated in this chapter—are important to effective leadership. Speaking actively and listening actively are physical and social demonstrations of what leaders must do in order to gain the hearts and minds of their followers.

Self-Assessment: Leadership Communications

Good communication skills are essential to good leadership. Use this self-assessment to evaluate your ability to speak and listen effectively.

Leadership Communications Assessment					
1. My people think that I am clear and concise in my communications.	①	②	③	④	⑤
	①	②	③	④	⑤
2. When I listen, I really listen— looking to ask questions and clarify the point the speaker is making.	①	②	③	④	⑤
3. Listening is one of the most important things I do.					
	①	②	③	④	⑤
4. Words are important, but actions speak more loudly.					
	①	②	③	④	⑤
5. My people want someone to listen to what they have to say.					
	①	②	③	④	⑤
6. Participation in a conversation can mean just listening attentively.					

*1 — Strongly Disagree   2 — Disagree   3 — Neutral
4 — Agree   5 — Strongly Agree*

Rate Yourself

If you scored between...

26–30 Excellent leadership skills
25–20 Good leadership abilities
19–15 Learning to lead
  >15 Need improvement

Action Planner: Developing Leadership Communications

Communications cuts to the heart of effective leadership. The most effective leaders are those who take the time to listen to what their people are saying. This Action Planner will provide you with some ideas that you can use to improve your ability to speak more clearly and listen more actively.

Reflective Questions

1. Refer to your mission statement. See if you can relate it (without notes) to a friend. After you explain the statement, show it to your friend. Ask him/her to evaluate how accurate, precise, and clear you were.

2. Think of an example of a hard lesson learned as a child or young adult. Write it down in story form and practice telling it to people. Refine your words and your speaking manner as you go along. (Practice does make perfect.)

3. Listening is essential to good communications. There are some exercises you can do to refine your listening abilities. Pick a favorite song. Listen to the words again. In addition to the melody, listen to the way the singer phrases (adds meaning) to the words. Think of how you might verbally emphasize (or phrase) key messages in your own life.

4. Choose a short article from a magazine or periodical. Read it. Form a list of questions you might ask if you were a reporter. Then relate your question-making ability to your listening ability.

5. Ask your associates to evaluate your listening skills. Use the following questions as a guide

   • Are you asking questions of people with whom you communicate?

   • Do you rephrase their questions for clarification?

   • Do you maintain eye contact?

   • Do you demonstrate good listening skills?

   • Do you demonstrate the right body language for listening?

*The deepest principle in human nature
is the craving to be appreciated.*

MARK MCCORMACK

CHAPTER 7
Recognizing the Contributions of Others

The Recognition Factor

Sociologists tell us that money is a satisfier, not a motivator. Once I asked a plant manager, who was having trouble staffing his plant, if he raised the entry wage would he attract more workers. He shook his head. While he agreed that he might attract a few more initial hires, he doubted that many would stick with the work unless they found it meaningful.

There is a scene in James B. Stewart's study of insider trading, *Den of Thieves,* when a young trader becomes upset because he believes his annual bonus of $10 million is not sufficient. Ten million dollars is more than most of us will make in several lifetimes. For this young trader, the issue is not money itself, but rather what he perceives to be a lack of respect.[1]

Recognition is critical to self-esteem. Money is nice, sure. But once you establish a basis of monetary rewards, without the accompanying verbal and social affirmation, the employee will quickly become disgruntled and ask for more. Eventually, more will never be enough. Motivation emerges from within. It manifests itself as the inner drive for achievement and yes, recognition.

Seldom do people come right out and asked to be thanked, but almost everyone expects to be recognized appropriately for their efforts. Like students craving feedback in the form of grades, employees also want that pat on the back, the "atta-boy" from the boss that says they are doing a good job. Seeking a chance for personal recognition is why many of us are willing to devote extra hours to an important project. We want to be noticed for our hard work.

Yet too many supervisors simply fail to realize this. In fact, many managers are befuddled when their best workers quit. Their initial reaction is, "I thought he was happy here." When asked if the manager ever demonstrated any recognition of the worker's effort, the manager usually shrugs, "I didn't think I had to."

You as a leader owe it to your employees to recognize achievement. As many companies have downsized and pushed levels of decision-making lower, it is imperative that employees who do excel receive timely recognition and reward. This is important for three reasons. One, good companies want to encourage successful employees to continue doing a good job. Two, proper recognition sets up strong patterns of reinforcement that other managers will emulate. Three, it makes good business sense. Research into employee attitudes shows time and again that it is far less expensive to recognize and reward current employees than it is to recruit new employees. Eventually effective recognition and reward practices create a culture of positive reinforcement that permeates the entire organization.

So what are some ideas that enlightened leaders can apply? Try these five:

Make Recognition a Value

Leadership is founded upon a system of beliefs and values. Part of that value system is concern for the welfare of others; after all, leadership involves doing something for the benefit of others. Part of that caring must include recognition of the contributions of others. When you begin to recognize people regularly, you integrate it into your leadership style; in time it becomes part of your core value system.

Create a Culture of Coaching

All of us, including leaders, need nurturing if we are to achieve our potential. A good way to bring out the best in people is to coach them: provide advice, counsel, and constructive criticism. Coaching is "contagious." When subordinates see a leader coaching or mentoring, they often emulate the behavior. In this way, leaders not only coach individuals they create an entire organization full of coaches. Such an environment, or culture, encourages people to stretch themselves. Good coaches challenge their employees to try harder, to push themselves, and maybe even take risks. In the long run, a culture of coaching delivers two benefits: it encourages employees to excel and it pushes organizations to achieve their goals.

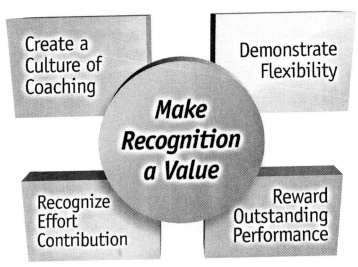

Recognition Model

Demonstrate Flexibility[2]

Most employees want to do good job, really. The more responsibility an individual has, the more likely she will make the job truly personal; she will live and breathe the business as if it were her own. At the same time, all of us have outside lives. Companies that understand their people have family and community obligations are companies that can attract and retain employees who are committed to their work as well as to their personal values. And in the end, isn't it better to have people with values than those who believe it is their duty to work like drones? I would argue that family-centered people are more productive than employment-centered people because they continually bring new perspectives gained from the outside world to their jobs. Their outside lives, instead of being a hindrance, become an enhancement. Furthermore, a worker who knows he will have time for his family is a worker who can devote his full energies to the job without worrying about family issues.

Recognize Effort and Contributions

People want to know they are doing a good job, so let them know. How? It is not rocket science. Write a memo praising an employee or a team and pin it to the bulletin board. Circulate the memo through e-mail. Some managers send thank you cards to employees, recognizing good effort. One manager I learned about sends notes to employees telling them how special they are. Recognition of this kind may seem a little mawkish to some, but guess what? It works. This particular manager works in a service business that is subject to high turnover. As a result of her efforts, she has reduced turnover and increased retention rates significantly. Put another way: the time it takes a manager to pen a personal note to a high-achieving employee is negligible when compared to recruiting and training a brand-new employee.

Reward Outstanding Performance

Reward, first and foremost, means increase in compensation. Employees who do a good job should be rewarded either with merit pay or a promotion, but sadly this is not always immediately feasible.

So what can you as a leader do in the meantime? Consider other forms of compensation. Grant comp time for employees who have put in extra hours. Or, give your hard workers tickets to the theater, movies, or local sporting events. Some generous employers have been known to spring for cruises or vacations for employees. [This is not the same as incentive trips awarded for specific goals; this reward is additional.] The extra measure demonstrates that you value the employees' commitment and want to keep them happy. Furthermore, such rewards create and solidify a culture of positive reinforcement.

Rewards may not come cheaply, but then again how much do you value good employees? Are you willing to go to the effort and expense of recruiting new workers? Consider the value of good ideas. Can you price them? What if one of them opens a new market, leads to the creation of a new product, or reduces your operating expenses? The cost of cruise—or a deck of thank-you notes—pales in comparison.

The most costly element of recognition, however, is not monetary. It is the investment of time, which is something most leaders have far too little of. Yet to ignore the contributions of employees risks far greater costs: loss of enthusiasm, motivation, and commitment. When an employee no longer cares, he is no longer productive, and that is a cost no leader can afford to bear.

Still, if you look at the list of suggested recognition behaviors closely, you will note recognition need not be costly. Valuing employees—and in the process providing coaching, flexibility, and recognition—is not a budget item; it should be a way of doing business that in the long run will pay back to the organization far more than it takes. When all is said and done, leadership is not about cost, it is about creating a culture where people feel valued and appreciated. No leader can argue against that principle. [Note: If none of these recognition efforts are in line with your management style, find methods that do. The point is to be proactive. Think about recognition in creative ways.]

Rewarding Yourself

Recognition of others is essential to effective leadership, but do not make the mistake of losing yourself in this equation. You work hard; you deserve some attention. After all, if you do not take care of yourself, who will?

Just as you reward your people, take time to reward yourself. Here are some things you might consider:
- Treat yourself and a special loved one to a weekend away
- Indulge a weekend in your favorite hobby: golf, skiing, tennis, boating, lounging
- Pick up a book for fun and read it.
- Buy yourself some new clothes; appearance can improve attitude.

Recognition as Affirmation

It is human nature to want to know how we are doing in a job. Feedback is essential to cultivating performance. Positive feedback is a form of recognition. It may or may not lead to reward.

Recognition is a basic leadership attribute; and in my opinion, it is the easiest to practice. Why? Because it is so simple. All it takes is a kind word here, or a pat on the back there. Recognition is simply the awareness of someone else; it is affirmation of personhood. Recognition communicates that a leader acknowledges the contributions of others, and in that way it is precious in simplicity and priceless in value.

And somewhere within the process of recognition there needs to be an acknowledgement of yourself as a leader. You must believe in yourself and your abilities to communicate with, care for, and guide others. The ultimate reward from self-recognition is the belief in self—the "yes, I can" that inspires others to follow you.

Self-Assessment: Leadership Recognition

Recognition is critical to a leader's ability to inspire others to follow. Use this self-assessment to rate your recognition skills.

Leadership Recognition Assessment					
1. It is important to let people know that you value their contributions.	①	②	③	④	⑤
2. People who work with me think that I share credit.	①	②	③	④	⑤
3. Recognition leads to ownership.	①	②	③	④	⑤
4. Leaders can create win-win situations so that individuals can take pride in their accomplishments.	①	②	③	④	⑤
5. Proper coaching can uncover and develop essential personal skills.	①	②	③	④	⑤
6. I reward myself for milestones of achievement.	①	②	③	④	⑤

1—Strongly Disagree   2—Disagree   3—Neutral
4—Agree   5—Strongly Agree

Rate Yourself

If you scored between...

26–30   Excellent leadership skills
25–20   Good leadership abilities
19–15   Learning to lead
  >15   Need improvement

Action Planner: Making Recognition a Habit

Recognition is essential to leadership, but how many times have we overlooked the contribution of others? This Action Planner will help you develop a plan to recognize your people in meaningful ways and in the process make recognition a habit.

Reflective Questions

1. Write a thank you note to a mentor. Include all the things you want to say. You need not send it but make a list of the benefits.

2. Make a list of all the people who make a contribution to your business. Write down what they do and make a point of thanking them. (If you are not in a leadership position, you can make a list of those who are helping you advance in your career. Again, thank them for their contributions.)

3. Make a point to do something special for each person who contributes. Among the suggestions are:

   • A dinner for two

   • Movie tickets

   • Flowers

   • Tickets to a sporting event or theme park

   • A "pass" to leave work early one afternoon per week for one month

4. Make a note to say thank you to one person on your day planner.

5. Take recognition home. Compliment your spouse, a friend, or even your child for something he/she did that made you happy.

6. Make a list of your accomplishments for the past five years (You'll be surprised at all that you have accomplished.) Think ahead to the next five years and write down what might occur, and then figure out ways you may reward yourself and your family for your effort.

*Leaders can accomplish little
without understanding and engaging
the qualities of the heart.*

DANIEL GOLEMAN

CHAPTER 8
Demonstrating Leadership Emotions

Leadership and Emotion

The success of a leader depends upon vision, competence, and expertise. Most importantly, however, it relies upon a leader's ability to connect with followers. This connection is founded ultimately upon the leader's understanding of the needs and aspirations of followers as well as the leader's capacity for empathy for those followers. Any study of leadership, therefore, should take into consideration the psychological underpinnings of the leadership contract, which itself is based upon communications, empathy, and self-knowledge.

A good place to begin a discussion of leadership psychology is with the renowned scientist of human behavior, Abraham Maslow. Dr. Maslow formulated the triangle depicting the hierarchy of human needs.[1] At the base of the triangle are physiological needs, such as food and safety. As you move upward, you pass through psychological needs such as a sense of belonging, love, and esteem. At the peak of the triangle is self-fulfillment, the capacity to achieve one's potential by exerting a sense of autonomy, responsibility, and achievement. This is the area in which leaders reside.

David McClelland, author and researcher, takes a different view, building in part upon Maslow's higher order needs. According to McClelland's research, individuals have three needs:[2]

- *Achievement*—need to set goals and accomplish them.
- *Affiliation*—need to be with people.
- *Power*—need to exert control.

Each of these aspects can be measured through surveys and assessments. Leaders, as you might expect, score well in achievement and power, but lower in need for affiliation. This discrepancy may account for why some leaders are able to make the tough decisions despite the fact it may cause human hardship, e.g., plant closings, downsizing, layoffs, and personnel decisions.

Maslow and McClelland are only two of many prominent theorists who have posited ideas on the psychological aspects of leadership. Another theorist who has studied leadership is Harvard psychologist Howard Gardner, a pioneer in the field of multiple intelligences. According to Gardner, there are at least seven intelligences: verbal/linguist, logical/mathematical, musical/rhythmic, visual/spatial, bodily/kinesthetic, interpersonal, and intrapersonal.[3] The fact that intelligence can be conceived and measured as a collection of different abilities permits us to consider ourselves and our personalities as a complex, yet interdependent, collection of diverse attributes.

Two of Gardner's multiple intelligences—personal and social—have led to the exploration of emotional intelligence, or as it is called, EQ. There is a saying among human resource managers: "IQ gets you hired, EQ gets you promoted."[4] Intelligence—an individual's ability to absorb information, synthesize it, and problem solve—is essential to leadership, but mental horsepower is not enough. What may be more important, however, is emotional intelligence, a concept pioneered by Daniel Goleman in his book, Emotional Intelligence. In fact, emotional intelligence may play a more important role with leaders than it does with other individuals because leaders accomplish their goals through the actions of others. If a manager cannot connect with his people on a personal level, the performance will suffer because people will simply be going through the motions.

According to Goleman, there are five aspects to emotional intelligence. All of them are inter-related and so it is important to understand what each one is and how it contributes to the whole.[5]

Self-Awareness: Know Yourself and Your Ability to Make Decisions

Who am I? It is a question we likely ask ourselves periodically throughout our lives. Aspects of our answer will change according to our life stage. When we are students, we may answer the question with a response that denotes our need to acquire an education. As first-time parents, we may respond that we are caregivers responsible for the needs

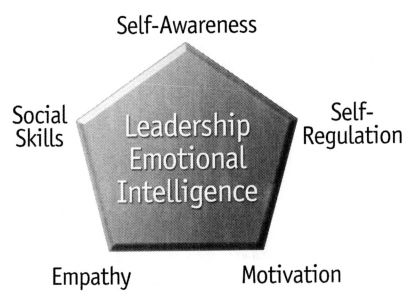

Leadership Emotional Intelligence
Adapted from Daniel Goleman, 1998.

of a child. As middle-age career persons, our answer may balance concerns with work with concerns for family.

The important lesson to learn from the "who am I?" question is self-knowledge. If you understand that you are a person who validates himself through work, then you need to put yourself in a position where you can achieve. By contrast, if you have outside interests that are more important than your work, you owe it to yourself to create an environment where you can pursue those interests in harmony with your work.

Self-awareness also influences your ability to make good decisions. It is essential to understand that your personality influences how you make decisions. If you are an empiricist, you will make decisions based upon facts. If you are a people person, you will make decisions based upon human factors. When you know the criteria by which you make decisions, you will be better able to make the right decision at the right time.

Self-Regulation: Controlling Yourself

Self-control goes hand-in-hand with self-awareness. Self-knowledge includes an understanding of feelings, in particular a management of those feelings. Leaders may show emotion, of course, but they are wise to keep those emotions in check, or at least well under control. If you are prone to overreacting, it would be wise to learn self-control techniques to alleviate those feelings. The last thing a leader can afford to do is "fly off the handle." Remember the Biblical example of King Herod and John the Baptist. Herod's temper tantrum cost the sainted wanderer his head.

Controlling emotions extends beyond anger; it includes the management of every kind of feeling—joy, sadness, anxiety. Followers expect a leader to be even-handed. It is acceptable to show emotion; in fact, a leader who does not demonstrate any emotion would strike most people as cold or indifferent. Likewise, a leader who arcs between emotional highs and emotional lows would be viewed as unstable, even unreliable. While we want our leaders to show that they are human, we need them to be in control.

Motivation: Inner Drive and Persistence

Self-control leads naturally to a sense of inner direction. Effective leaders often seem as if they are guided by some internal compass. The force driving this kind of compass however is not magnetic, it is motivational. Motivation emerges from within an individual; it cannot be imposed by an authority figure. Different factors motivate different people. Motivators, according to McClelland's research, vary from individual to individual.[6]

Achievement motivated individuals:
- Are willing to do their best
- Want to exert personal responsibility
- Desire to achieve
- Seek innovative solutions
- Require feedback

Power motivated individuals:
- Desire to influence others
- Seek to have their ideas predominate
- Like to give advice
- Place a high regard on position and status

Affiliated motivated individuals:
- Want to be liked
- Desire warm, friendly relationships
- Need to belong to groups

These examples of motivating factors are by no means complete. You can no doubt come up with factors of your own. Looking at this list you can see that motivation emerges from the individual, but leaders can inspire it by establishing an environment where the individual can succeed. Good leaders do this by creating "win-win" situations for people to demonstrate that they can achieve and by doing so gain confidence in their abilities. The sense of satisfaction that arises from this situation will give the employee confidence to continue to achieve. This achievement instills motivation.

Furthermore, competition among peers can be used to create a climate of achievement. But leaders must be careful to channel internal competition in ways that benefit everyone without marginalizing the few. For example, in competitive situations wise leaders are careful to recognize everyone for their efforts, but savvy enough to reward those who deliver the results. So while some internal competition can be destructive, when managed properly it can produce greater levels of performance.

Empathy: Understanding Another's Feelings

Knowing oneself can lead to a greater understanding of others. In fact the better we know ourselves it is likely the better we will be able to assess the feelings of others. True self knowledge includes an awareness, or what author-psychologist, Ellen Langer, calls "mindfulness"—a state of paying attention to the needs of others.[7]

Self-knowledge also is an acknowledgement of limits. Even if you may be the shy, retiring type, acknowledgement of that fact will enable you to manage your feelings and in turn learn to deal with others. Not all of us can be "touchy-feely" people. Nor should we be. Our personalities are formed early on; our challenge is to learn what our feelings are so that we can display them appropriately and in the right situations.

Social Skill: Interacting with Others

Getting along with other people is essential to effective leadership. A leader should not be a buddy. Leaders have to make tough decisions that might conflict with friendship. But it is important that a leader inspire confidence and trust in followers. Trust can only come if the leader conducts herself with honor and integrity.

At the same time, leaders need social skills to be able to interact with others. Many great generals in history from U.S. Grant to Dwight

Eisenhower possessed the common touch; this common touch emerged from their modest upbringings. Grant and Eisenhower regarded themselves as soldiers first, officers second. With that mindset, they were able to converse with their men as men, not as leaders to subordinates. This sense of familiarity not only inspires confidence in men, it enables the leader to gain insight into the mood and mindset of his people.

Good corporate leaders do the same. They remember what it was like to work for someone else and use the power of their personalities to put people at ease so that they find out what is going on. Most importantly, they work hard to learn what they need to do to help individuals grow, develop, and contribute more effectively.

Leaders Know Themselves

Knowing yourself—your abilities, your feelings and your relationships with others—is essential to effective leadership. The most effective leaders are those who understand themselves as individuals. They know their capabilities and their limitations. Good leaders will then seek out people who possess different talents and skills that complement themselves as well as the entire organization. A confident leader can feel self-assured enough to give authority to individuals who can do the job.

Managers who feel threatened by competent subordinates are destructive and must be removed from positions of authority because they can do the organization great harm. The wise leader understands that life is a series of limitations. The wise leader understands her personal shortcomings and can use the knowledge of them to empower others to do what she herself cannot do.

Coming to grips with your emotional intelligence is essential to effective leadership; it becomes a gateway to greater understanding of yourself and your ability to relate with others as an individual, a colleague, and a fellow human being.

Author's Note: *Howard Gardner also has written an excellent study of leadership entitled* Leading Minds. *The book profiles twelve different leaders and categorizes their leadership abilities according to a capacity to envision a future, live by example, and to transcend their field. Among the leaders cited in the book are Pope John XXIII, George C. Marshall, and Margaret Mead. Certainly these three lived their vision and used their lives as examples for others.*[8]

Self-Assessment: Leadership Emotions

In order to be an effective leader, you must have the ability to get along with others. Use this self-assessment to rate your interpersonal skills.

Leadership Emotions Assessment					
1. I know my abilities and my limitations.	①	②	③	④	⑤
2. Leadership requires making tough decisions and sticking to them.	①	②	③	④	⑤
3. My people believe that I control my emotions well.	①	②	③	④	⑤
4. As a leader, I must create situations and opportunities that will motivate my people to succeed.	①	②	③	④	⑤
5. I make the effort to understand the background and circumstances of the people around me.	①	②	③	④	⑤
6. The ability to "go along" depends upon your ability to "go along" with people.	①	②	③	④	⑤

1 — Strongly Disagree   2 — Disagree   3 — Neutral
4 — Agree   5 — Strongly Agree

Rate Yourself

If you scored between...

26–30 Excellent leadership skills
25–20 Good leadership abilities
19–15 Learning to lead
>15 Need improvement

Action Planner: Implementing Leadership Emotions

Getting along with people is essential to effective leadership. This Action Planner will help you create a plan to develop your interpersonal communication skills so that you get along with people more effectively.

Reflective Questions

1. It has been said that you must know yourself before you know others. Take a moment to create a personality inventory listing your traits and tendencies. [There are no "right" or "wrong" answers.]

My Personality At Work	That's me	That's me sometimes	That's not me
1. I am generally optimistic about my work.	◯	◯	◯
2. I enjoy the company of others.	◯	◯	◯
3. I prefer to work alone.	◯	◯	◯
4. I try to look for solutions rather than blame.	◯	◯	◯
5. I like to get to know people before I work with them.	◯	◯	◯
6. I do not see the need of getting to know people.	◯	◯	◯

2. After you complete the profile. Ask yourself if you are happy with this picture. If not, consider ways to maintain your strengths and improve your weaknesses.

3. When you become hot under the collar, consider implementing one of the following methods to cool down:

   • Walk away from the situation for a moment and take a deep breath

   • Listen to soothing music

   • Exercise

   • Write down what is bothering you and devise a possible solution

   • Talk out the difficulty with people you trust

   • Try to take the "big picture" i.e., life is short and this situation will pass?

4. Make a list of what motivates you. Think about how you might translate your motivators into opportunities for others.

5. Think of an example of persistence in business or in sports. What do you think enabled that organization (or team) to persevere and eventually succeed?

   • Vision

   • Planning

   • Communications

   • Teamwork

   • Reflection

6. Make a list of the people with whom you interact at work. Write down one salient fact about that person that is a source of personal pride for each of them. Make a point of engaging them in conversation about it.

Colleague	Trait	Comment

> *There is nothing permanent*
> *except change.*
>
> HERACLITUS

CHAPTER 9

Learning to Be a Change Leader

Leadership for Change

At its core, leadership involves movement either of people or ideas. Inherent in movement is change. And every effective leader needs to recognize that things do not remain the same. Not ever.

So what does the effective leader—one who knows himself and has the proven ability to lead—do? Embrace the challenge and realize that many of today's solutions are for yesterday's problems. Just as the generals of World War I fought that long bloody struggle with 19th century tactics, today's business leaders too often fight their battles with mental models more suited to another era. General Motors, Sears, and Xerox all faced this dilemma in one way or another in the early 1990s until a new leadership team took over. We must consider new ideas as a means of facing of new challenges.

To make change work for the organization, a leader must do three things:

- Commit to change
- Commit to continuous learning
- Commit to leadership

Commit to Change

If Franklin Delano Roosevelt were alive today he might say, "The only thing we have to change is change itself." And he'd be right. It is axiomatic that we live in an era of change; what may not be so clear is the fact that we must "change the way we change." [1]

It makes sense. If everything we know is evolving—the market, our organization, our people, our society—then it makes sense that the transformative processes themselves must be undergoing changes.

Consequently, we must find new ways to deal with change. The task of managing change falls, of course, to our leaders.

It has always been so. Thomas Jefferson, one of our Founding Fathers, lived in an era of extreme change. He helped draft the Declaration of Independence, served as America's representative to France just prior to the French Revolution, and more than doubled the size of the United States with the Louisiana Purchase in 1803. Most importantly, Jefferson helped usher in the Age of Republicanism in the New World. Consider Jefferson as chief agent provocateur of change. In the early 19th century, as historian Stephen Ambrose writes, Jefferson became intrigued with the changes that would occur with balloon travel.[2] In an era when the fastest travel was by horseback, Jefferson understood implicitly that travel through the air would mean an end to geography as the formidable barrier to communication and commerce. Furthermore, Jefferson understood that the balloon would accelerate the pace of change. That pace has seemingly accelerated ever since.

Today's business leaders do not have Jefferson's luxury of time and distance. Events that occur half-way around the world can have immediate impact. For example, whenever there is a shift, upward or downward, in any of the capital markets around the world, it nearly always produces some kind of movement on the U.S. capital markets. Global businesses must develop strategies and skills to address changes in technological, market, and consumer environments. Businesses in telecommunications must keep their collective antennae tuned to changes in computer software, cable television, public utilities, and market demands.

What can companies that thrive on change teach us? The skills for anticipating, managing, and embracing change.

The Change Process

Anticipate Change

Look outside of your business for cues of impending change. Strategist Gary Hamel advises businesses to examine changes that occur outside of their arena to see what impact they might have on their business.[3] By observing how different businesses deal with change, managers might learn lessons applicable to their own organizations. For example, Hamel informed a group of telecommunications executives that they had nothing to teach each other. He advised them to spend their time getting together with people from utility and financial service companies. Ideas arising from those multidisciplinary exchanges would benefit all three businesses. Value would emerge from the diversity of experience as well as the variety of different viewpoints.

Manage Change

Develop mechanisms for integrating change into the organization. Focus on developing communications tools: email, websites, and regular meetings to discuss rapid developments. Tune the organization to a sense of nimbleness so that when change does occur, it seems normal, rather than discontinuous.

Embrace Change

Understand that change is a reality and that in its wake lies opportunity. Dispense with the fear; welcome the possibilities. Encourage people to view change as a breath of fresh air that can invigorate old thinking and open the windows to new thought. How can a manager do this? By fostering a culture that anticipates and manages change.

All three of these methods of meeting change have a common element: leadership. But again, the leadership itself must be supple enough to flex with the change process, yet firm enough to remain true to the ideals of the organization.

Commit to Continuous Learning

The best way to anticipate change and embrace it is through learning. Learners are those who are in a state of perpetual preparation as they acquire new skills and seek to implement them.

Most good leaders are good learners. Why?

- One, they are curious. Like great white sharks, they prowl the seas of change looking for new information.
- Two, again like sharks, they devour information when they get it, making a hearty meal of it.
- Three, leader-learners use this information to help them navigate new paths through ever changing waters.

Leaders who value learning are patterning themselves on the "learning organization." The term implies a commitment to helping individuals and teams grow collectively and systemically so that they become smarter, wiser, and more competitive individually and collectively. No organization can become a learning organization without the commitment and support of senior management. Leadership is essential to instilling a shared vision that will enable individuals and teams to develop their potential and share their lessons throughout the entire organization.

Put another way, if one area of the company discovers a better way of doing things, or happens upon an interesting piece of research that works, it would be helpful to the entire organization if everyone in the company could share in the new ideas. In part, this is what it means to be a "learning organization"—sharing ideas, concepts, successes with others in the organization. The other part involves people coming together for a common purpose and learning to solve their problems in a logical, systemic way.

Learning organizations may more aptly be called "highly performing organizations" because improving performance is the end goal of learning within an organizational framework. In fact, many people working in the field prefer the latter term because it differentiates itself from training. Training, of course, is a part of learning, but only one small aspect of it. What is important is the sharing of ideas and willingness to work together to find new solutions to emerging challenges.

The leading thinker in the area of organizational learning is Peter Senge. "Through learning we re-perceive the world and our relationship to it," writes Senge. "This then is the basic meaning of a 'learning organization'-an organization that is continuously expanding its capacity to create its future." [4] In his book, *The Fifth Discipline,* Senge identifies five disciplines necessary for organizational learning: systems thinking, personal mastery, mental models, shared vision, and team learning. These five disciplines work together holistically to enable individuals and teams to learn in ways that are healthy, sustainable, and nourishing for the entire organization.

For the sake of simplicity, we can boil the five disciplines down to three areas: personal development, team growth, and systemic learning.

Organizational learning must occur on the personal level first and foremost. The individual must commit to a vision as well as to a means to make it happen. The team (or the organization as a whole) has to work together to fulfill its goals. And both individuals and teams must be rational and logical in the way they apply the learnings of the past and present throughout the entire organization (systemic) to generate results for the future.

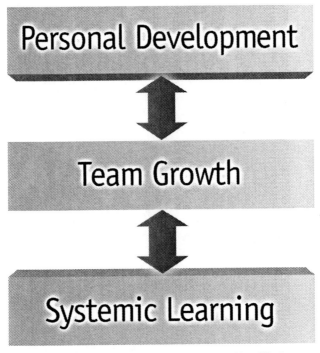

An Organizational Learning Process—Simplified
Adapted from The Fifth Discipline *by Peter Senge, 1990.*

If you're reading this and asking: "What's all this got to do with me? I'm paid to manage not educate. I can't be worried about this stuff?" Think again! Organizational learning is fundamental to an organization's ability to profit and grow. Why? Profitability depends upon a company's ability to produce goods and services with a sufficient margin to ensure a stable operation, a healthy, safe environment for employees, and an ability to put away some for the development of future goods or services. Organizational learning will enable people within the company, as individuals and as teams, to observe their roles, note their contributions, learn from their mistakes, and forge new ideas and new products for future. This in turn leads to growth, the ability to increase in size, scope, and return. Failure to tap into individual, collective, and systemic thoughts will doom a company to run circles around itself because it will never put the knowledge it has to good use. Consequently, employees will have to re-invent the wheel with every new project.

Leaders, by contrast, need to understand that organizational learning does not by itself guarantee profit and growth. But organizational learning does provide the disciplines a leader can use to find out what's right, what's wrong, and build on the rights to create a strong, competitive enterprise. Leadership based upon continuous learning is leadership positioned for growth and opportunity.

Commit to Leadership (Change + Learning)

Since our world is one of continuous change, we must learn to integrate change throughout our organizations. How? Through leadership. Leaders must champion change. Whether you need to develop a new product, revamp your compensation system, or change your culture, it will not occur without the support of senior leadership. Leaders can champion change by anticipating it, managing it, and embracing it. And they must ensure that change takes hold within the organization by committing the organization to a continuous learning process.

Change is never easy; it also is disruptive and messy, but it is necessary to the health and success of an organization. Commitment to change requires a commitment to leadership.

Self-Assessment: Leading Change

Leadership requires an ability to adapt to change as well as to hold to one's convictions. Use this self-assessment to rate your leadership skills in these areas.

Change Leadership Assessment					
1. Adapting to change may require a change of position.	①	②	③	④	⑤
2. When a tough situation arises, I step forward to offer my ideas.	①	②	③	④	⑤
3. Tough decisions require toughness and the courage of conviction.	①	②	③	④	⑤
4. Leaders may not be liked, but they need to be respected.	①	②	③	④	⑤
5. Learning begins with a commitment to gain new information and a willingness to use it.	①	②	③	④	⑤
6. Leaders are responsible for creating an environment where people can learn individually and collectively.	①	②	③	④	⑤

1 — Strongly Disagree   2 — Disagree   3 — Neutral
4 — Agree   5 — Strongly Agree

Rate Yourself

If you scored between…

26–30 Excellent leadership skills
25–20 Good leadership abilities
19–15 Learning to lead
>15 Need improvement

Action Planner: Learning to Change

Leading people is about leading change. This Action Planner will help you develop a mindset that is attuned to changing situations so that you can prepare yourself and those you lead to adapt to the changes and embrace the opportunities.

Reflective Questions

1. Everyone says that life is a constant series of changes. Take a moment to review the transitions in your own life.

   • High School

   • College

   • First Job

   • Marriage

   • Children

   • Career Choice

2. Consider those transitions. What circumstances did you experience that caused you to alter your path?

3. More and more, educators are considering learning a life-long process. Consider ways you can improve your learning skills.

   • Read books

   • Seek out a mentor

   • Change careers

   • Go back to school

4. Think of ways you can become an agent of change:

   • On the job: seek new responsibilities, seek new ways of doing things, new ways for your employees to develop their skills.

   • At home: look for ways to improve family togetherness.

   • In the community: become a volunteer.

5. One of the best ways to prepare an organization for change is to encourage people to become active participants in the learning process. Look at your organization. Consider ways you can enable people to learn by themselves as well as together in teams.

   Individually

   • Distribute self-improvement books.

   • Sponsor web-based training.

   Collectively

   • Arrange for employees to attend the same training course.

   • Consider team-building activities.

   Organizationally

   • Ask teams to share their lessons learned with other teams.

   • Create a website devoted to "best practices."

6. Leaders play an integral role in fostering a culture of learning. Think of the good teachers you had in high school or college. Consider adopting some of their teaching methods when you teach your people.

   - What type of teaching method did they apply? (Lecture, discussion, hands-on activity, or various combinations of these three.)

   - Why did you find this method an effective way to learn?

   - How can you apply this teaching style to your own people?

   - How would your people benefit from having you as a teacher?

> *One must know oneself before knowing anything else. It is only after a man has thus understood himself inwardly and has thus seen his way, that life acquires peace and significance.*
>
> SØREN KIERKEGAARD

CHAPTER 10
Reflecting on Leadership

A psychiatrist, an internist, and a surgeon are duck hunting. A duck flies overhead. The psychiatrist says, "It looks like a duck. It sounds like a duck. But I can't be sure." The duck flies past. Another duck flies overhead. The internist says, "It flies like a duck. It looks like a duck. I think." He fires and wings the duck. Another duck comes into view. The surgeon blasts away. As the duck flutters to the ground, the surgeon mutters, "That's a duck!"

React now. Think later. That's how many managers are taught to behave when it comes to making key decisions. If it looks promising, go for it. Don't wait to be told to do something, just do it!

This "do it now" attitude is to be expected; it's the way many of us are educated. The public education system, as Peter Senge points out in *The Fifth Discipline,* measures us on the basis of results, not knowledge per se. We attend class. We study. We take exams. We move on. More often, the emphasis in education is placed upon gathering and digesting information rather than developing critical thinking skills. So when a youngster grows up, it's only natural she will favor action over reflection.[1]

This trend, however, can be dangerous. How many times do we see groups formed quickly without much thought to given to setting objectives, obtaining necessary resources, or even getting the right people together? As a result, half way through the project, the team disintegrates because it did not have the right resources to enable the right people to do the job. These problems result from a lack of forethought as well as lack of reflection. Managers feel compelled to act quickly simply for the sake of moving and as a result, they fall into traps. Before they can have time to reflect on the current problems, another crisis arises. And so it seems that organizations lurch from crisis to crisis without taking time to reflect on the causes and problem-solve solutions.

Not only can problems occur from actions taken too hastily, they can occur from inaction. Three notable examples come to mind. One is the decision by Swiss watch companies to ignore the logic-based timepiece. Even though the instrument had been developed at Neufchatel in Switzerland by Swiss engineers, Swiss management could not envision a world of watches without moving pieces. Their individual and collective mental model (a term that refers to personal perception, or individual world view) would not stretch to accommodate this technology. As a result, the Japanese and Americans developed watches and calculators with the same technology and the Swiss watch industry was decimated for decades.[2]

A second example shows a similar lack of foresight, which might have been prevented by reflection, which occurred when IBM initially ignored the significance of the PC revolution. It would be logical to think that a computing company would embrace new technology. IBM managers by contrast dismissed the micro-processor-based technology because their mental model (along with their sales and profits) were tied to large-scale, centralized computing systems. The idea of individual computers scattered throughout a company was antithetical to them.

In a third example, in the early 1990s, Motorola was a world leader in analog cell phone technology. When the shift to digital cellular communications began, Motorola was slow to change over. As a result, it missed the opportunity to convert existing analog customers to digital as well as win new digital customers. Motorola then suffered significant financial losses.

The point is not to bash the Swiss, IBM, or Motorola. Hindsight is 20/20 after all, but disastrous decisions of the future might be precluded if managers were encouraged to integrate reflection into their business model. And in the case of IBM and Motorola, they were able to right their ships when their senior leadership reflected on the situation and consequently began to make the right moves.

Consultants Michael Hammer (co-author of *Reengineering the Corporation*) and Steven Steadman (co-author of *Start Controlling Your Destiny...or Someone Else Will*) believe organizations need to make "reflection" a part of the work process.[3] The authors define reflection as a means of examining and assessing every element of the work process in a systematic way. Hammer and Steadman offer six applications (or "tasks") for reflection that should be integrated into the work environment. These applications range from examining external factors such as the environment, the competition, and the customer to gaining a better understanding of the company itself.

The culminating task for Hammer and Steadman is "assumption breaking;" this activity brings the entire reflection process together. "Collecting new information by itself leads nowhere; it is in the nontraditional thinking of assumption breaking that its value is realized," say the authors.[4] Breaking assumptions forces organizations to address the serious issues facing them such as developing new strategies, implementing new technology, or developing new markets. Questioning the status quo can be laborious, even painful; but it is only through a willingness to take the time to look at everything through fresh eyes can an organization truly discover what is best for them, now and in the future.

Reflection is critically important, to be certain, but how can managers learn to reflect? In *Hope Is Not a Method,* Gordon Sullivan and Michael Harper (both retired U.S. Army officers) tell the story of Hal Moore, an Army lieutenant colonel, who used the power of reflection to his advantage during the first major clash between U.S. forces and regular army units of the North Vietnamese Army. U.S. Army infantrymen were outnumbered by four or five to one. As the fierce battle raged, Moore asked himself these three questions over and over again: What is happening? What is not happening? What can I do to influence the outcome?[5]

His responses to these questions helped him develop the strategy and tactics to keep his men resisting and the enemy at bay through extremely heavy fighting. While Moore's troops suffered heavy casualties, the toll may have been much higher had it not been for his willingness to think of ways to protect his men under fire.

Leaders can apply the same questions to themselves and their organizations.

- *What is happening?* How is my company doing in the marketplace? Why is this so?
- *What is not happening?* What areas are we deficient in and why?
- *What can I do to influence the outcome?* What avenues (e.g., strategies, technologies, markets) can I suggest to make our company more competitive?

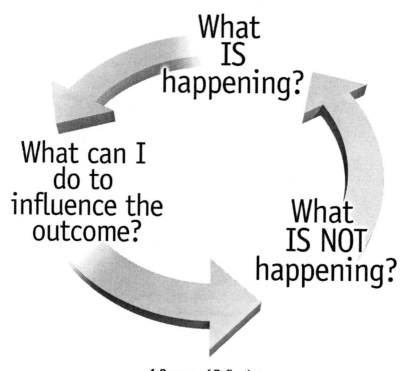

A Process of Reflection
Adapted from Hope Is Not a Method *(Sullivan and Gordon, 1998).*

The answers to these questions will lead to some surprising insights. Leaders should ask themselves these questions repeatedly, as well as encourage their colleagues and subordinates to do the same.

Using Reflection to Anticipate the Future

Reflection is one technique that leaders can employ to help their organizations become true "learning organizations"—one that gathers and learns from its past and current experiences in ways that prepare it to face future challenges with preparation, strategy, and proper foresight. Reflection also can nurture the leadership process because it is a "time out" from the day-to-day process. It enables the leader to draw perspective on where she has been and where she is today.

Reflection also is a necessary tool to look ahead. At first blush, "looking back" to "look ahead" may seem contradictory, but it is not if you think about. Two reasons. It is a truism that history is a preparation for the future; or as we say today, "What goes around comes around." By looking at our past, as well as our present, we can predict where our future might be. We, of course, will not know with certainty, but I think it is safe to say that we can assess the trends that will affect us.

Two, the willingness to examine the past puts one in a contemplative state of mind that leads to the formation of "what if?" questions. By examining the past it is natural to think about what happens next. Reflection enables us to examine current trends and wonder if they will continue. If they do, we can decide how we must respond.

At the same time, reflection prepares us to accept discontinuous change, i.e., an interruption that alters everything after it. You can think of the invention of the microprocessor as one such example. It opened up the development of the personal computer, enabling access to information to anyone within an organization. The microprocessor altered the balance of power within an organization and thereby changed history.

Few people outside research labs, if then, could have predicated its impact, but reflection or the willingness to ask "what if" questions prepares one for the potential of change.

Reflection as an Active Process

Leadership by nature is an active process. It requires an individual to "move" a group of followers (either physically, emotionally, or spiritually) from one place to another. Action is inherent, surely; but from time to time leaders (as well as everyone) need to take the time to slow down and examine themselves and our organization to see if the direction we are headed is correct. Reflection—taking time out to ponder the past, the present, and the future, and the leader's role in it—is essential to effective, responsive leadership.

Authors Note: *Hal Moore and Joe Galloway have written movingly of the 7th Cavalry's battle with the North Vietnamese in the Ia Drang Valley in their book,* We Were Soldiers Once...And Young.[6]

Self-Assessment: Reflection Skills

Leaders must periodically take stock of themselves and their situation to gain perspective. Use this self-assessment as a means of reflection.

Leadership Reflection Skills Assessment					
1. Self-knowledge is essential to self-growth.	①	②	③	④	⑤
2. An unexamined life is a life without purpose.	①	②	③	④	⑤
3. I make time to think what I can do to influence outcomes.	①	②	③	④	⑤
4. Willingness to reflect leads to willingness to change.	①	②	③	④	⑤
5. I encourage my people to take time out to reflect on their current situation.	①	②	③	④	⑤
6. Reflection on where I am today will enable me to predict where I might be in the future.	①	②	③	④	⑤

1 — Strongly Disagree   2 — Disagree   3 — Neutral
4 — Agree   5 — Strongly Agree

Rate Yourself

If you scored between...

26–30 Excellent leadership skills
25–20 Good leadership abilities
19–15 Learning to lead
  >15 Need improvement

Action Planner: Reflection

Reflection is that process by which we take a step back and assess the situation and our role in it. This Action Planner will help you develop skills for reflection that you can use to evaluate your ability to reflect.

Reflective Questions

1. Put reflection into practice. Begin setting aside 15 minutes per day to reflect (a.m. or p.m.). Call it your own personal time out. Shut your office door. Take no phone calls. Focus on your goals. Look ahead (or back on) the day and use the Reflection Model (described below). [If you like, you may go for a walk instead of staying in your office.]

2. Create a journal of your thoughts and important actions. You may make entries during your reflection time, but do not write during the entire period. You need your thinking time. Periodically review your journal; with the benefit of hindsight, consider what you did right and what you might have done better.

3. Apply the Reflection Model to your personal life.

- What is happening? How am doing in my home life? Why is this so?

- What is not happening? What areas am I deficient in and why?

- What can I do to influence the outcome? What can I do to improve my situation to make my home life better?

4. Apply the Reflection Model to your professional life.

- What is happening? How is my company doing in the marketplace? Why is this so?

- What is not happening? What areas are we deficient in and why?

- What can I do to influence the outcome? What avenues (i.e., strategies, technologies, markets) can I suggest to make our company more competitive?

5. Apply the Reflection Model to your future.

- What is happening? What I am doing today to prepare for my future?

- What is not happening? What decisions am avoiding now that may affect my future? Why I am I avoiding making those decisions?

- What can I do to influence the outcome? What must I do to prepare myself for the future?

> *The recipe for success is, first [make] a reputation*
> *for creative genius; second, surround yourself*
> *with partners who are better than you are;*
> *third, leave them to get on with it.*
>
> DAVID OGILVY

CHAPTER 11

Supervising and Leading Others

Supervising others. It's a task that every manager faces. In fact, it is the essential role of management, and certainly of leadership. How well you supervise determines how well you can lead. Leadership is about creating followership. But you will not have followers if you cannot supervise properly. Rick Snyder, former COO of Gateway the computer company, asserts that the most difficult task in management is not becoming a senior executive; rather it is assuming that first supervisory role.

Entrepreneurs learn early on that you must let go in order to soar. In other words, as the business grows managers must learn to cede control to others. Instead of do-it-yourselfers, managers must become supervisors—enabling others do the work.

Many successful leaders look back on their early days in management and shake their heads at their early missteps. Invariably they tried to do too much, too soon. This behavior is natural because most often managers come from the ranks of achievers. They are accustomed to doing whatever it takes and more to succeed. Application of those traits is necessary for solo achievement, but may be a prescription for disaster when supervising others. Performing the task and simultaneously supervising is folly and will lead to failure as well as the alienation of many good, hard-working individuals.

There are things, of course, you can do to prepare yourself to supervise.

Supervising Guidelines

Set Expectations

It is human nature to want to know the type of person for whom you work. The best way leaders can communicate their personality and

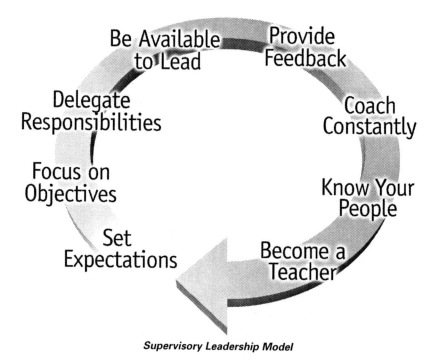

Supervisory Leadership Model

behavior to their subordinates is by setting expectations—what I expect you to do and how I expect you to do it. The "what I expect" will come from business objectives. These are typically straightforward; the how I expect involves attitudes, responsibilities, and behaviors. If you want your people to be bright, cheerful, and energetic, you need to be clear in your expectations.

Focus on Objectives

Supervisors establish objectives for their people. The strategy may come from senior management, but it is the supervisor who translates it into tactical commands. For example, if the strategy of a company is to increase market share, it will fall to the marketing department to find ways to grow it. For example, a brand manager will write the objectives for her people to execute. The manager will delineate the tasks—developing advertising, budgeting media, creating promotions.

Delegate Responsibilities

Few jobs within an organization can be accomplished without assistance; they require the leadership of one, but the participation of many.

Leadership is the "hand" on the tiller; but the skipper knows there are many "hands" on the deck—e.g., hoisting the jib, straightening the mainsail, organizing the ropes, and manning the winches. The captain is the leader; he delegates tasks to the crew. Or in the case of our brand manager, she will decide which members of her team will do the budget, advertising, and promotions. Ideally, the decision about who will do what will be shared between leader and direct-reports; shared decision making is another form of delegation.

Delegation is not easy. For supervisors, it is the necessary "leap of faith" that followers will do the job. In time, supervisors learn that their own success depends upon the success of their people, and they will do whatever they can to provide support in the form of resources, manpower, tools, equipment, and of course, advice.

Be Available to Lead

Supervision requires letting go so the work can begin, but leadership requires interest and a willingness to become involved. Think of "being available" the way you might envision your time management. You want to be a master of detail, not a servant to it. To be a master, you must let others do their jobs.

Your involvement will be dictated by circumstance. If the project is going well, you may need only to be kept informed of its progress. If the project encounters crisis, you may wish to step in and take a more "hands-on" approach until the situation is resolved. Be aware, however, that all crises do not require supervisors to intervene. Many issues can be resolved with the employees at hand; let them exert their responsibility and take control.

Judging your need for involvement will take time and practice. A first-time supervisor will be tempted to jump in and take over at a moment's notice, i.e., every time a light bulb needs changing. Veteran leaders pick their moments. When Skip LeFauve was heading Saturn, he was a master at being available, but not intervening. Like a parent, you need to let your people know you care, but that you have faith in their ability to succeed.

Provide Feedback Continuously

"How am I doing?" That question served as a mantra for Ed Koch when he served as mayor of New York City in the 1980s. Koch used the question to gauge the mood of his constituents and their reaction to him and his programs. Likewise, your people want to know what you think of them. It is human nature; we humans like to please. You owe them your assessment of their performance Do not wait until an annual performance appraisal. You want to give an employee time to correct a deficiency, or continue a positive behavior. Schedule one-on-one time on a regular basis. You can also do it informally.

Instruments such as the 360° evaluation, where managers are evaluated by their subordinates, peers, and supervisors, can be invaluable because it gives the manager a more complete picture of how she performs with different groups. Such feedback can illuminate our "blind spots"—those deficiencies about which we are unaware. For example, if someone believes he is a good communicator, but in reality keeps things close to the vest, feedback can shed light on the problem. A good leader will then make an effort to improve and be more open in his communications.

Coach Constantly and Consistently

All of us need advice and counsel in the ways of our jobs. Leaders have a responsibility to their followers to provide that assistance on a regular basis. The easiest model to understand is the sport's coach; styles differ. Some coaches take the role of the caring uncle, dispensing words of advice with the proverbial arm around the shoulder. Other coaches take the "in your face" approach going nose to nose with their players and screaming at the top of their lungs. When dealing with adults, however, the more avuncular approach works better. None of us likes to be screamed at, particularly if our performance has been sub-par. On the other hand, we need coaches to provide encouragement and recognition for good effort and good work.

Know Your People

Every supervisor must make time to become acquainted with his people. It goes beyond just first names, but rather knowing who they are as people and what their strengths and weaknesses are and what motivates them. Good supervisors take the time to learn what kinds of work individuals like to do; some may like prescribed tasks with definite beginning and ending points; others prefer open-ended assignments that call for creativity and intuition. A supervisor's ability to match assignments to work-style will do wonders for productivity as well as morale. But such an ability depends upon a supervisor's willingness to learn about his people through conversation, question, and informal investigation. Taking time to know people upfront will deliver benefits during the job assignment.

Become a Teacher

Effective teaching requires personal commitment. Good teachers do not simply tell; they show. For example, if you must instruct someone on how to operate a piece of machinery, tell them how first, then demonstrate, then observe them do it several times. This kind of learning is experiential; i.e., hands-on. It is only one way to learn, but it is an effective model for adults. Whether you are teaching an employee to operate a back hoe, or design a media event, the same principles of telling, showing, and observing apply. Effective supervisors are teachers who demonstrate the how-to, but also live their message and their expectations through their behaviors.

The Challenge of Supervision

Supervision is not limited to the eight steps listed in this chapter. It encompasses the sum life experience of an individual as well as all of the leadership behaviors like vision, communications, and recognition. John Gardner, the noted author on leadership, cautions leaders from trying to do too much. "If the leader is a visionary with little talent for practical steps, a team member who is a naturally gifted agenda-setter can provide priceless support." According to Gardner, the best leader is one who makes certain that the team has the right mix of skills and talents.[1] In truth, supervision is a balancing act because it requires "letting go" as a means of taking charge. The more effectively you can channel your leadership energy into supervision the more effective leader you will become.

Self-Assessment: Supervising Your People

Your people will enable you to become the leader you are capable of becoming. How well you meld your abilities with theirs will determine your effectiveness as a leader. Use this assessment to see how you are supervising your people.

Leadership Supervisions Assessment					
1. I regard my people as my most valuable resource.	①	②	③	④	⑤
2. My expectations of others are clear and precise.	①	②	③	④	⑤
3. My people believe that I establish attainable objectives.	①	②	③	④	⑤
4. Delegation is essential to effective leadership.	①	②	③	④	⑤
5. Taking time to coach someone may be time well-spent in achieving department objectives.	①	②	③	④	⑤
6. I would like to think that others regard me as a teacher.	①	②	③	④	⑤

*1 — Strongly Disagree   2 — Disagree   3 — Neutral
4 — Agree   5 — Strongly Agree*

Rate Yourself

If you scored between...

26–30 Excellent leadership skills
25–20 Good leadership abilities
19–15 Learning to lead
  >15 Need improvement

Action Planner: Supervising Your People

Supervising people may be the most difficult task in your leadership repertoire. You cannot do everything necessary to succeed. You need to take time to delegate and at the same time set reasonable expectations for your people. This Action Planner will help you determine your objectives, your expectations, and your willingness to delegate. When you supervise correctly, you become a teacher and mentor that your people will want to follow and for whom they want to do their best.

Reflective Questions

1. Make a list of the business objectives for which you are responsible.

2. Identify people on your team to whom you can delegate tasks and responsibilities.

3. Describe the work environment you would like to create as a leader.

   • How do you want your people to regard work?

   • How do you want your people to treat one another?

   • How will you help your people get necessary resources?

4. Consider ways you can be available to lead. Note: These efforts also will enable you to get to know your people better.

   • Hold agenda-less meetings to discuss a work situation.

   • Keep the door to your office open.

   • Hold regular pizza break meetings.

   • Hold an off-site luncheon meeting once per month.

   • Consider occasional socializing after-hours.

5. Determine ways in which you can provide feedback to your employees.

   • Schedule regular one-to-one meetings once every two months.

   • Meet for a coffee during work time.

   • Call an individual into your office.

6. Identify your favorite "coach." [In this instance, coach may be anyone who provided guidance in a particular activity, e.g., drama, voice, computer, sports.]

   • What makes this coach effective?

   • What does this coach do that you can emulate? (Vision, plan, communicate, recognize, etc.)

   • How can you take the lessons of this coach and apply them to your work environment?

> *The strength of the group*
> *is the strength of the leader.*
>
> VINCE LOMBARDI

SUMMARY

Personal Leadership

If you have read everything to this point, you are indeed a patient and precise reader. You have my undying gratitude. But, if you are like me, and like to skip from chapter to chapter, sometimes in no particular order, here's a handy wrap-up that will serve as a summary to the entire book.

Essentials of Personal Leadership

Personal leadership is a matter of moving from the "I can" to the "I will." It contains three core elements:

- Autonomy: the willingness to lead others.
- Initiative: the willingness to take action, to make something happen.
- Responsibility: the willingness to be accountable for consequences.

Personal leadership is:

- Centered on values
- Outward directed
- Tempered by the courage of conviction
- Liberating

Defining Leadership Character

Leadership character is the sum of personal values, conviction, and compassion, leavened with humor. Character is comprised of:

- Personal values
- Conviction that drives decision-making
- Willingness to change
- Compassion
- Sense of humor

Defining Leadership
Character

Supervising and
Leading Others

Creating
Leadership Vision

Reflecting on
Leadership

**Personal
Leadership**

Developing
Leadership
Strategy

Learning to
be a Change
Leader

Maximizing
Time to Lead

Demonstrating
Leadership
Emotions

Communicating
Leadership

Recognizing the
Contributions of
Others

Cycle of Personal Leadership

Creating a Leadership Vision

Personal vision is rooted in the character of the individual. If a leader is to be successful, he must create a vision that does the following:

- Focus on goals
- Tap into aspirations
- Adapt to change
- Share with others
- Lead others to inspiration

Developing a Leadership Strategy

The leader must develop a personal strategy by implementing the following:

- Vision. Knowing where you want to go
- Objectives. What you want to do when you get there
- Long-term Plans. Finding ways to get there over time
- Short-term Plans. Finding ways to get there now.
- Win-win Situations. Give yourself a chance to celebrate
- Re-Vision. Prepare yourself to do it again

Maximizing Time to Lead

Leaders must gain control of their time; it may be their most precious resource. To manage time effectively, it is necessary to:

- Set priorities
- Implement 80/20 rule
- Master the details (Don't let them master you.)
- Cut the fluff
- Make time for yourself

Communicating Leadership

Leaders need to employ active speaking and active listening skills:

To speak actively...

- Think aloud
- Be clear and consistent
- Practice aloud
- Engage physically
- Listen
- Tell stories
- Apply humor

To listen actively...

- Approach with an open mind. (Don't pre-judge.)
- Ask open-end questions (Those that begin with words like how, why, tell me.)
- Maintain eye-contact (People want to see you.)
- Engage your body. (Uncross your arms, relax your muscles, animate responses facially.)

- Listen to what the other person is saying. (Think before you reply.)
- Empathize with the situation. ("This reminds me of this situation that happened to me once...")
- Rephrase what the other person is saying. ("If I understand you correctly, you are saying...")
- Participate in the conversation. (Serve and volley; serve and volley.)
- Repeat the entire cycle until the entire session is concluded.

Recognizing the Contributions of Others

Effective leaders recognize and reward their followers for their outstanding efforts.

Consider:

- Make recognition a value
- Create a culture of coaching
- Demonstrate flexibility
- Recognize effort and contributions
- Reward outstanding performance
- Rewarding yourself

Demonstrating Leadership Emotions

All forms of intelligence are essential to leadership, but emotional intelligence may play a more important role with leaders than it does with other individuals because leaders rely upon their ability to interact with others. Psychologist, Daniel Goleman, identifies five aspects to emotional intelligence.

- Self-awareness: Know yourself and your ability to make decisions
- Self-regulation: Controlling yourself
- Motivation: Inner drive and persistence

Achievement motivated individuals:

- Are willing to do their best
- Want to exert personal responsibility
- Desire to achieve
- Seek innovative solutions
- Require feedback

Power motivated individuals:

- Desire to influence others
- Seek to have their ideas predominate
- Like to give advice
- Place a high regard on position and status

Affiliated motivated individuals:

- Want to be liked
- Desire warm, friendly relationships
- Need to belong to groups
- Empathy: Understanding another's feelings
- Social Skill: Interacting with others

Learning to be a Change Leader

Leaders, by nature, are called upon to lead people through change. To do so effectively, the leader must:

Commit to change

- Anticipate change
- Manage change
- Embrace change

Commit to continuous learning

- Emphasize personal development
- Foster team growth
- Employ systemic learning

Commit to leadership

- Lead the change process

Reflecting on Leadership

Leaders must take time to renew themselves through contemplation and reflection. Here are three questions you can ask yourself:

- What is happening?
- What is not happening?
- What can I do to influence the outcome?

Supervising and Leading Others

Supervision is leadership; it is when the leader within becomes the leader of others. To become an effective supervisor, it is necessary to:

- Set expectations for followers
- Focus on organizational objectives
- Delegate responsibilities
- Be available to lead
- Provide feedback regularly
- Coach continuously
- Know your people
- Become a teacher

PART **2**
How Others Lead

Stories from the Front Lines
of Leadership

JAC NASSER
Leadership in Motion

How do you transform the world's second-largest company into an organization where everyone feels as if he or she owned the company and acts accordingly?

That question forms the challenge that Jac Nasser has undertaken as he strives to convince everyone within Ford Motor Company to regard the Company as if it were their own business. That goes for everyone—from himself (the CEO) to the new hire on the assembly line—all 335,000 employees.

Entrepreneurial Leadership

Nasser is direct is his expectations for his leadership. "Most of all, I want [our people] to think like owners of a business. And as Ford shareholders, most of them are. I also want them to think about how best to maximize shareholder value. If a decision is not right for the customer, it cannot be right in the end for the shareholder. I also want them to think about growth. Profitable growth. That means both new businesses as well as improving our share in segments of the market where we haven't done as well as we should."

This personal sense of ownership—another word is "shareholder value"—is not a buzzword Nasser picked up from today's flavor-of-the-month management class. It is in his blood. He is the son of a Lebanese immigrant to Australia who arrived with nothing but his wits and built a series of businesses. Today Jac confesses with wry amusement that his father does not think his son has really made it because he didn't build the business himself. "My father thinks that anyone who goes to work for someone else is a failure." [1]

Teaching Leadership

From his family as well as his own experience, Nasser knows what it means to run your own business. As a teenager he started a bicycle shop and a car repair business; both failed. On his third try, he was successful as the owner/operator of a coffeehouse.[2] It is this sense of entrepreneurship, coupled with a can-do spirit, that Nasser is determined to instill in each Ford employee. Jac's approach is novel even by today's standards of "hands-on" management. To persuade employees of the urgency of the moment, Jac has become a teacher, personally lecturing to more than 50,000 Ford employees about business leadership and shareholder value. His lectures (themed around what Ford calls the Business Leadership Initiatives) are down-to-earth, inside glimpses into the whys and wherefores of Ford strategies, coupled with an urgent call-to-action on the need to exert a sense of personal ownership of the business. What's more, Nasser insists that all managers throughout Ford become teachers, too. His own example serves notice that no manager is above teaching. By having managers teach subordinates through every layer of management, Nasser helps to make certain that themes and messages are not simply communicated but become part of the way Ford conducts itself as a business, employer, and corporate citizen.

The commitment to teaching is central to Nasser's leadership. He confesses that throughout his years in management he had been teaching; he simply didn't call it teaching. Now he does. "Once you start to teach in-house with your own people leading the effort, the teachers themselves have no choice but to behave differently. You've gotten up in front of your people, and you've said, 'This is what I believe. This is how we should run the business.' After [that has occurred] it's very hard to disown yourself from the change process. You have to live it and breathe it every day. Teaching enforces the discipline of change."[3]

As part of the Business Leadership Initiative, Jac is helping to forge a new culture. To get things started, managers have been assigned short-term projects, nearly 5,000 in total, that will help them develop quick solutions to nagging issues. For example, one team of engineers is working on ways to eliminate excess noise from the best-selling Ford F-150 pickup. Their solution was to install a cross-member. Another team was charged with reducing costs of engineers visiting plants during manufacturing launches; their solution was to rent apartments, use company-owned pool cars for transportation, and use cell phones to avoid hotel charges. Most of the projects are small in nature, but each one is important to the overall health of the company. More importantly, by accomplishing these short-term gains, the participants feel a sense of accomplishment that they can take pride in, particularly when tackling the big issues that always arise.[4]

And getting more personal as well as socially minded, Nasser encourages his managers to become involved in community service projects as part of the Business Leadership Initiative. Projects have ranged from cleaning up parks to painting public buildings. The exercises have a strong team-building component to them, but also they underscore Ford's commitment to the community. Not everyone was excited by the prospect of volunteer work. "It was a challenge to us," confesses David Murphy, vice president for human resources. "Some resisters did try it and wrote back saying, 'This is great.'" [5]

Global Leadership by Experience

Jac Nasser is not your conventional executive; for starters, Jac has spent less than a third of a thirty-year-plus career at Ford in the United States. Fortune magazine calls him the "consummate insider-outsider...an import...and therefore an unusual candidate to run an American icon [Ford.]" [6] One is tempted to say that Jac is a high-compression bundle of incredible energy and zeal, but that term hardly describes the man. He is a man of purpose and activity, but there is no wasted motion. He does not sprint down hallways; he does not jump on desks. He does not wave his arms. He simply achieves.

Leadership is a topic that Nasser exemplifies rather than philosophizes. But when asked, he is very clear about the qualities necessary for a leader. "Leadership is first, integrity. If you don't have integrity, what do you have? High standards of performance would be another aspect of leadership. The auto business is tough, and it takes hard work and a commitment to high performance standards to succeed. Frankness and openness are two other [leadership qualities]. I want a free exchange of ideas and a debate that brings out all sides of an issue. Finally, passion. Some call it a 'fire in the belly.' Whatever the phrase, you have to love what you're doing. Love the product. Love the business. Love beating your competitors. Love making a difference for your company, its customers, and the employees whose livelihoods depend on it."

Leadership Drive

Of course, one place where you might find Jac channeling his physical energy is at Dearborn Proving Ground, putting some new vehicle prototype through its paces. Behind the wheel Jac is fully engaged and fully alone: no phones, no memos, no email. He is in charge, truly immersed in the job at hand. Seeing him drive is to gain an insight into his inner drive (no pun intended). He is focused and intense—listening, probing, and searching for clues into the vehicle's performance.

It is not unlike what he does back at the office. Jac is a man on the prowl, looking not for faults, but for solutions, ways to do things better. Jac is engaged and on a mission. Nearly nine decades after Henry Ford implemented the scientific management methods of Fredrick Taylor, Jac Nasser is updating the approach. "We have undertaken a scientific way of running the business differently," says Nasser. "And it won't stop." [7]

His early reputation was that of a cost-cutter. In fact, Jac once told the media that he had never missed a cost objective and did not intend to begin now. The result was $11 billion removed from future vehicle development costs, and many more billions trimmed from day-to-day operational costs.

But Jac knows better than most executives that cost cutting will only go so far. Quality is a prime concern, but Nasser realizes that quality—nearly zero-defect quality—is only an entry into the competitive arena. You can also be fast to market, quick to respond to consumer trends. But improving the cost-quality-speed triad is only a starting point. After the costs come down, the quality goes up, and speed sizzles, you still need something else—creativity and passion for the business.

The Human Face of Leadership

Nasser values the human element. He doesn't make speeches about the need to streamline organizations or "empower" people: Jac simply does it. He is a man of action, of urgency, of the moment. He cherishes the creative spark. He likes to give his direct reports room to maneuver and to innovate. As long as it is within the dictates of Ford strategies, no one will ever run foul of Jac.

One of the common misapprehensions that young managers often may have is that senior managers ascended almost godlike into their current positions, without having made their share of career blunders. When Nasser speaks informally to internal audiences, he is candid about his early career. "Like most managers, I made many mistakes." He also quickly learned how to make the best of bad situations. "Early in my career, I was transferred from Australia to the Philippines to manage the Ford operations, which were losing money at the time and, most likely, would have to be closed. I soon learned that I was chosen because senior management thought I couldn't make the situation any worse! We were strapped for cash and couldn't pay our suppliers or even our taxes to the government. We issued a kind of promissory note—in reality, an "I-owe-you" note—until we had the cash. But the experience taught me a great deal, and I learned quickly. By the time I left several years later, we were operating in the black."

What does Nasser look for in the executives he hires? "A number of things, but first and foremost teamwork. You can have the most brilliant, technically proficient managers, but if they are not committed to the team, great harm can be done to the organization. Next would be a global mindset, knowledge of the business as a total enterprise, and willingness to embrace change as the only constant we can count on."

Part of his insight into people, as well as the global market, stems from his background as a global businessman. While some executives talk about opening new markets in Asia or Latin America, Jac has already been there decades ago. As a result, Nasser is a multi-linguist (English, Arabic, French, Spanish, and Portuguese). A true globalist, he is very much at home in the world of business anywhere in the world. His multicultural outlook is not an affectation; it is his humanity, as well as his way to do business.

For this reason, Jac champions diversity, not as a management fad, but as a matter of human dignity. As a young Lebanese immigrant to Australia, Jac certainly must have felt the sting of being an outsider, particularly in the predominately Anglo-Aussie culture of the Fifties and Sixties. But instead of becoming bitter, Jac became better; he has risen to the top, but he has not forgotten his heritage, or the values of hard work and entrepreneurism that have made him the man he is today. For him, diversity is also good for business.

Communications is essential to effective leadership. "I think at Ford we do a better job than most. I write a weekly note, *Let's Chat About the Business,* that's distributed electronically. The responses have been terrific. I read every one. Beyond *Let's Chat,* there's a company wide survey that employees are invited to complete that covers a broad range of topics. The feedback from these surveys is very helpful in measuring morale and commitment to our objectives. But most important, I try to get out as much as I can and talk directly with employees, answer their questions, and teach them the business."

When situations dictate, Nasser can be very much a hands-on manager. "One technique I use to enhance cross-group teamwork is to get leaders to work together on specific assignments. Instead of talking about teamwork, put people in situations that demand it. You take two or three people, or a small team, and give them a real-world problem to solve that forces them to work together. They get to know one another and trust one another's judgment."[8] Nasser continues this theme. "If I could eliminate the organizational chart, I would do it. It is archaic. It doesn't reflect the consumer organization. It doesn't reflect the way an efficient enterprise should run."[9]

Pursuing the Vision

Nasser has a sixth sense about the future of the automotive industry. "We're going to see sport utility-type vehicles on car platforms—vehicles that are somewhere between a sport utility, a minivan, and station wagon. It's going to be difficult to make an extremely sharp distinction between cars and trucks—there will be a blurring."[10] But that's just for starters. After all, this is a man who stood up before an industry conference packed and said "Sometimes we act as though we are in the internal combustion engine business. We're not. We're in the personal transportation business."

Under Nasser's leadership, Ford established a visionary new brand, the Think Group, which he says, "provides innovative, environmentally friendly solutions for personal mobility." The Think product line will include a battery-powered urban car, a low-speed golf-cart type vehicle, and even a bicycle. In addition, Ford is active in the development of hybrid vehicles that combine an internal combustion engine with an electric power source as well as fuel cells that burn hydrogen and produce water as exhaust. "Since its inception, our Company has been a leader in automotive technology and innovation," says Nasser. "That same spirit of innovation drives us today...[and] is proof that personal mobility and environmental responsibility can co-exist."

At another industry gathering in Detroit, he postulated about the future of the automotive industry as it enters the 21st century. To Nasser, the old ways of doing business, creating products and hoping customers will buy them, is over. Today's automotive business model calls for something more creative and intuitive. He would like to transform Ford into "a superior customer-driven company that produces automotive products and services." What does this mean? It means that Nasser has a vision of Ford as a company in touch with its consumers' rational and emotional needs for personal transportation, but also one that is creative and intuitive about how to satisfy those needs with new products that excite and delight customers.

Getting closer to the customer is a prime reason why Nasser has embraced the Internet as an essential way of doing business. Ford took a leadership role in the formation of Covisint, an Internet venture that links automotive suppliers together with automotive manufacturers in a kind of cyber community that will not only reduce costs, but also improve learning and customer responsiveness. As Nasser explains, "Business cycles of the 1980s had a life cycle of two or three years. We are now in online business models...[This cycle] is going to be driven by the softer side of the business, by a team that has leadership and edge and that understands the global trends around the world and is able to adapt those into the business model." [11]

Creative Escape

It is no wonder with his mind set on the future that you can find him at peace also in the design studio, reveling in the colors and shapes of tomorrow, and as he likes to say, the "smell of the clay." This is Jac at his best. The tinkering uncle, a sort of modern-day Walt Disney, happiest when he is surrounded with designers, peppering them with questions and challenging their answers.

He takes the same inquisitive mode to his office. Jac in a meeting is a cross between absorbing information faster than might seem humanly possible then pulling from the depths a question or a comment that might bring the whole issue—or decision—into sharper focus.

Importantly for a leader, Jac has won the admiration of his competitors. An executive at BMW calls Jac a "charismatic leader with lots of ideas and enthusiasm." Robert J. Lutz, a long-time automotive executive, says "Jac used to work for me [at Ford], so I know him for what he is—an exciting and brilliant automotive executive and unconventional thinker." [12] Others concur. In 1999, *Automotive News,* a leading trade publication that covers the automotive industry, named Nasser "Industry Leader of the Year."

Leaders as CEO

As CEO and President, Jac, and Bill Ford, Jr., Chairman and great-grandson of Henry Ford, form a unique management team. As Ford says, "I will run the Board, Jac will run the Company." Jac points out that while the role of non-executive chairman is uncommon in the U.S., it is much more common in Europe, and he is quite comfortable with it. Most importantly, the two men have forged a partnership in leadership that will allow the two of them to complement one another. Bill Ford represents the continuity of tradition and family, while Jac Nasser represents operations and enterprise. Skeptics say two men of power cannot co-exist, but that statement underestimates the capacity of both men. Both are deeply committed to the future of the Company. While Ford has blood ties to the company, Nasser's ties are almost as binding. Ford Motor Company has been his career since he graduated from the University of Melbourne in 1968.

Two events that occurred within a week of each other demonstrate what kind of CEO leader Nasser is. The first was Ford's high-profile acquisition of Volvo cars. While such an acquisition had been rumored for months, Nasser had kept mum, ruling out nothing in public with the statement, "everyone is talking to everyone" referring to larger automakers discussing mergers with smaller ones. It later came out that Jac had been working behind the scenes for months meeting with representatives of Volvo. Such stealth, coupled with a near reverential praise of Volvo design and automotive integrity, demonstrate Nasser's love of the business as well as his passion for doing things correctly, properly, and with due respect for all parties. In fact, as an indicator of Nasser's respect to Ford's newest subsidiary, he appeared at a joint news conference the day of the announcement with Volvo's Chairman Carl Lindquist in Gottenberg, Sweden, home of Volvo's corporate offices. Bill Ford handled U.S. media chores in Dearborn. [Again, the power of the team demonstrates how leadership can be in two places at the same time.]

The second event happened the following week. A boiler room at the Rouge Plant, Henry Ford's dream plant for turning raw materials into fully assembled cars, exploded and injured scores of workers, including six fatally. Nasser was in Europe. Upon his return a few days later, he immediately went to the hospital to check on the condition of the survivors. When interviewed by the media, his face betrayed his fatigue, but his emotions bubbled to the surface saying that the workers were part of the Ford family, and it was his responsibility as a corporate officer to do what he could to help. [It should be noted that Bill Ford was in town on the day of the accident. Upon learning of the accident, he immediately raced to the plant, offered support to the victim's families, and hours later visited the injured in the hospital. In this regard, both Ford and Nasser, individually and collectively, demonstrate the very human side of leadership.]

Together Ford and Nasser are leading the Company toward a new economic model, one that embraces what is known as the triple bottom line: economic vitality, environmental compatibility, and social responsibility. Both understand that if Ford is to remain a leading company it must make vehicles that produce fewer emissions, are more fuel efficient, and are continually safer for drivers, passengers and other vehicles on the road. In July 2000, Ford Motor Company committed to improve the fuel efficiency of its sport utility vehicles by 25% by 2005. In a speech at the National Press Club in Washington announcing the plan, Nasser said, "This fuel economy commitment is good for our business, will provide a cleaner environment, and is a good thing to do for society." Nasser added, "This is a voluntary commitment, but one which I and every member of the Ford team stand behind."

All of what Nasser is pushing Ford to achieve underscore his commitment to improving shareholder value over the long term. That challenge remains Nasser's mission. It is what shapes his inner self as a corporate leader. And lest you think that it is simply a dollars and cents equation, Jac knows better. When you convince employees to take responsibility for the business "like a store owner turning off the lights at night to save money" they begin to act as personal owners of the business.

Challenging Others to Lead

The secret of Jac's leadership style, if there is one, is unlocking the potential of the individual to create a new kind of company where people can fulfill their objectives as they build an enterprise that increases in value as it enriches their personal sense of mission. It's a mean trick to do when you are an entrepreneur building from scratch, but the task becomes just that much more arduous when you are running a nearly century-old organization layered with tradition and bureaucracy.

Jac cherishes tradition. He collects watches, loves opera, and collects vintage vehicles. As a man who has spent thirty years trotting the globe for the Company, he values the legacy of Ford Motor Company and all that it means, the world over. It is bureaucracy—and all its multiple reviews—he abhors. Jac likes to remind people of his time as the head of Ford of Australia. "In those days, we could get all the key people in the company around a conference table."

Harnessing Supervisory Talent

Nasser understands that his success, and that of Ford Motor Company, depends upon its employees. "We have a tremendous source of talent and energy available. I'm not sure we've been successful in capturing it and putting it to work as effectively as we could have. If we miss our goal of becoming the world's leading auto company, it won't be because of a lack of talent. Because the caliber of the women and men of Ford around the world is top notch. If we miss our goal, it will be because senior management, for whatever reason, did not use this talent to its fullest potential. That's the challenge for me and the team who will lead Ford into its next century."

To get Ford's 335,000 employees around a table may be physically impossible, but with Nasser's boundless energy—and his commitment to using communications technology—if anyone can do it, he can. "It's important to stay quick and nimble, and create a spirit of entrepreneurship throughout the company." [13]

That's leadership, and that is Jac Nasser's mission in motion.

───────────

In the late summer of 2000 as this book went into publication, news of problems with Firestone tires on Ford Explorer was making headlines. Under pressure, Firestone agreed to recall more than 6.5 million tires, many of which were standard equipment on the popular Ford Explorer. The recall was prompted when suspect tires unexpectedly shredded causing the vehicle to rollover.

As Ford's CEO, Nasser assumed the prime leadership role in Ford's handling of the rapidly unfolding Firestone crisis. Soon after, Ford began sharing all available tire data as well as communicating what it knew about the nature of the problem and the extent of all possible damages.[14] The company also assembled a team of experts dubbed the "tire team" to coordinate resources and problem-solve issues related to the recall. Nasser met with the team on a daily basis.

Getting the outside perspective is essential to a leader in a crisis situation, so Nasser conducted his own information search, entering chat rooms on the web and posing as a customer on Ford's own call center. Nasser also contacted the CEOs of other tire manufacturers to arrange for increased production of replacement tires.[15] As part of the communication effort, Nasser appeared in television commercials explaining Ford's plans for the recall and reiterating *its commitment to putting the safety of its owners first. Additionally, Ford stopped production of new Explorers to divert all available tires to the recall, a move that cost the company an estimated $30 million per week.*

Later Nasser testified in front of Congress, displaying his usual tenacity and toughness, promising that such mistakes would never happen again. The day after the initial hearings, Nasser held an impromptu meeting of Ford employees in order to thank publicly those who were working around the clock hours to help with the recall. During the meeting, Nasser himself received a standing ovation from Ford employees as well as the very public endorsement of Bill Ford who praised Jac's strong leadership style and personal commitment. "Nobody," said Ford, "could have done a better job than Jac Nasser."

What the American public witnessed during the crisis is what those inside Ford have known for years. When problems arise, Jac Nasser has the inner drive and personal passion to do whatever is possible to find solutions that are in the best interests of the customer and ultimately the people of Ford Motor Company.

RED BERENSON
Portrait of a Coach as a Leader

The first thing that strikes you about meeting Red Berenson for the first time, aside from his red hair, still vibrant with color in his late fifties, is his shyness. Looking at the man you would never guess that he played seventeen years in the National Hockey League, played on a victorious Stanley Cup team, and now runs arguably the most successful hockey program in college hockey.

What would not surprise you after talking to him is this: Red was the first college player in history to go directly from college to the NHL. In 1962, armed with a degree in business administration from Michigan and one of the fastest backhands in all of hockey, Red joined a storied hockey franchise—the Montreal Canadiens. It was his backhand quickness that helped him score an amazing six goals in one game for the St. Louis Blues in 1968. [The all-time NHL record is seven goals.]

After his playing days, Red became a head coach of the St. Louis Blues where he gained NHL Coach of the Year honors in 1981. Following his time in St. Louis, Red became an assistant coach under the legendary Scotty Bowman, whom Red had played for in St. Louis.

While Red acknowledges picking up lessons from all of his coaches, it is Bowman, who has coached teams to eight Stanley Cup titles, whom Berenson credits with teaching him about the art of coaching. Mel Pearson, the associate head coach at Michigan, draws favorable comparisons between Berenson and Bowman. "They are so alike. Some people who don't know either Scotty or Red think that they are aloof or hard to approach, but underneath they are very caring, sincere people." Pearson continues, "Scotty is a very firm disciplinarian. And I think Red is, too."

After a long and successful career in professional hockey, Red was lured to his alma mater in 1985. The University of Michigan program that had nurtured him and had earned seven National Collegiate Athletic Association titles was in tatters. The championships were memories; and in some seasons, so were victories. In the years before Red returned, Michigan posted a string of back-to-back losing records. The hope was that Berenson would be the man to turn things around.

Beginning With a Sound Vision

Like most successful leaders, Berenson began with a vision: restore the greatness of a legendary hockey program. Having been a standout player in a standout Michigan team, Red was direct about what he expected for the program. "When I came here my biggest challenge was to get Michigan hockey to be like the way I thought it should be"—a return to its traditional strengths. "I remember saying in our first press conference, 'I want to change the image of Michigan hockey. I don't like what people are saying about our team and our program.' I thought Michigan hockey should be one of the most respected programs in the country year in and year out."

To do so, Berenson knew that he would have to recruit the best young players. His goal was straightforward; he wanted top recruits to say "Michigan" whenever they were asked to name a top college hockey team. Today that's a given; when Red started in the mid-Eighties it seemed a stretch.

But Berenson was not about to do it at the expense of scholarship. He himself was committed to education. During his pro career, Red used his off-season time to earn an M.B.A., likely a first for the NHL of his era, a time when most players turned pro before completing high school. Red's dictum was to strike a balance between good education and good athleticism, not an easy task. "I'll never forget when I first started, somebody once said, 'What's wrong with Red's team?' And somebody else answered, 'Too many students on the ice.' That bothered me, really bothered me." [1]

Berenson knew it would take time to recruit the right players to build the right team and eventually the right program. "He had a directive to rebuild Michigan hockey," says Keith Molin, a former associate athletic director. "But sometimes people are in a rush to build. He did it one brick at a time" [2] In fact, Berenson's teams logged losing records in his first three seasons. Pearson recalls those early days. "They used to give me a stack of 100 tickets and I couldn't give them away…It was tough those first couple of years. Red didn't like losing; none of us did." [3] It took Berenson's teams five years to make the NCAA playoffs, but since that time his record is impressive:

10 consecutive NCAA appearances
8 consecutive 30-game winning seasons
9 consecutive Great Lakes Invitational titles

5 outright Central Collegiate Hockey Association championships
2 of the winningest goalies in NCAA history back-to-back
  (Steve Shields 111 victories 1990–94; Marty Turco, 127 victories
  1994–1998)
2 NCAA Championships: 1996, 1998

And perhaps most impressively, under Berenson's leadership Michigan has posted the most victories and the highest winning percentage (0.768) of any collegiate hockey program in the country.

Setting Expectations

Berenson's vision for the program is rooted in his expectations for his players. "There should be a certain code of conduct that the players should live by without having any written rules." This unwritten code covers the way players "handle themselves, the way they go to school, the way they come down to the rink, the way they dress, the way they work on the ice, the way they present themselves as players and as people."

What's more, says Berenson "We want our players to make the school proud of them, make their families proud of them, make our team proud of them, make the coaches proud of them, and make each other proud."

Bill Muckalt, who played for Michigan from 1994–98 and served as co-captain on the 1997–98 NCAA championship team, said that Berenson expects his players not only to be good students, but also good citizens and role models for the community. Such behavior is part of the Michigan Way, which Muckalt defines as, striving for "the highest standard you can achieve, [to be] the best on and off the ice."

Berenson's expectations for his players begin during recruiting. He looks for men who are "clean-cut" and "bright-eyed." Furthermore, he looks for kids who will look you in the eye and are able to demonstrate leadership. He also wants kids who are coachable and are willing to work hard on the ice and at the books.

Having coached for so many years, Berenson admits that he can often tell if a player's attitude and personality will fit into Michigan as soon as he meets him for the first time. Yet Berenson is also a realist with a touch of mellowness. "Now, that doesn't mean that I am so narrow that I won't take a kid that is a little bit off the wall. I have had kids who went home in the summer, put their earrings in, grew their hair long, and seemed to do well. But, they were good kids. They had heart and soul. They worked their tails off. They were top students. I had no problems with them."

Berenson's expectations help shape his players for life after hockey. "I want each of them to be the kind of person that I would hire if I were the president of the company. And that takes into account not only any talent that they bring to the table, but the fact that they have a work ethic [as well as] a sense of commitment and responsibility."

Focus on School

Much of Berenson's approach to coaching involves keeping academics and athletics in balance. "I try and keep school and hockey in perspective. From time to time I will talk to our team about school, about attendance, about life after hockey, about getting something out of this and taking advantage of a school like Michigan before it is too late."

He makes liberal use of stories to make his points. "I will talk to them about former players that I knew who became hockey bums, never had an education, couldn't get a job. [By contrast] I talk to them about former players at Michigan who have done well because of their academic prowess and I try to establish to our team that the better you do in school, the better you will do on the ice. The two can go hand in hand."

Berenson enjoys citing the names of student-athletes who excelled on the ice as well as inside the classroom. "These are the guys who I respect the most...the ones who are doing it at both ends." He fondly recalls a hockey player who was not a star, but a solid all-round player. "He walked onto this team. He had a great four-year career and now he is in medical school. That is the kind of kid I think is a real hero."

Berenson demonstrates his commitment to academics where it affects him most—on the ice. If a player is not doing well in class, "I will give him a week off. In some cases I have pulled players...until they can show me that they are back on track at school. They may not volunteer," Berenson says with a wry smile, "but I will give them the time." The benefits of the off-time, according to Berenson, are two-fold. The player is given time to reflect on how much he misses hockey, and often comes to realize that he also can achieve in class if he applies himself.

Berenson will not turn a blind eye to poor academic performance even in the heat of competition. In Michigan's run to the championship in 1998, he benched Marty Turco, the NCAA's all-time winningest goalie, for cutting class. "It was an easy decision for me. [But] I didn't like the fact that it may have cost us first place, especially against [arch-rival] Michigan State."

Berenson went further. "The other thing I did was to make it clear to the media and to the world why we were doing this. I made it very clear why [Marty] was not playing because…it was the fans and everybody else he had to answer to." Berenson will never berate a player in public; and did not in this case, as he was careful to point out Turco's attributes as a player, person, and student. But standards are standards, and with Berenson, standards must be upheld.

Preparing His Team

College hockey has the longest season in collegiate athletics, stretching from practices in September until early April if the team goes to the NCAA finals. Mental preparation is essential. Just as in business, members of a hockey team come to understand that learning to deal with adversity is necessary for success. And contribution as a team is essential.

Berenson is low-key, but firm in his resolve. "You have to stay focused on how you come to the rink to play, how our team is going to play. If you are not prepared, you are not ready to play a real game." Lack of preparation will lead to unwarranted penalties, lackadaisical play, and easy goals for the opponent.

Inspiring Confidence

Preparation, however, will only take a team so far. Like all good coaches Berenson inspires his players to believe in themselves. "A coach has to give his team confidence." During a key game in Michigan's 1998 run for Berenson's second title, the team fell behind to North Dakota by two goals in the first period. Instead of dwelling on failure, Berenson and his coaches focused the team's energy on taking a positive view. This freed the players from getting down on themselves. "And so our kids went out and didn't worry about being behind; they just worried about playing well."

This comeback is all part of the Berenson legacy. Assistant coach Billy Powers credits Berenson with gift of inspiring a team no matter the score; by combining stories with tactical advice, Berenson can make his team feel that they can get back into a game, no matter what the score is.

"Red is an optimist. He never gets too down about any certain situation. Instead of worrying about what isn't going right, [Red] worries about what can we do to make it go right and get back in a game." Assistant head coach Pearson believes that Berenson's success as a coach can be found in his ability to look at the positives, make appropriate adjustments in personnel, and then let the players get on with the game.

Bill Muckalt, who won two NCAA titles under Red's tutelage, derived nearly as much reward from talking to the coach about the victory off the ice than he did winning it on the ice. "You want to impress him and earn his respect." By winning the second title, Muckalt says, "We showed him we could do it."

Constructive Criticism

The ability to inspire confidence requires a coach to know his players as individuals. At practice, Berenson likes to coach one-on-one: counseling, critiquing, cajoling. In addition to providing specific advice about how to improve an aspect of a player's game, Berenson is a master at getting a player to think more positively about himself.

Dealing with young players two generations younger than himself has given Berenson the wisdom of age when it comes to criticism. "I have seen kids that if you raise your voice, their head goes down and they are just devastated. I have seen other kids who don't hear you until you raise your voice and get in their face. I have seen kids who need to be stroked and told how good they are and how good they can be."

If an individual player is going "against the grain of the team," Berenson employs a two-prong strategy. He will either pull the offending player aside for a heart to heart, or criticize the player in front of the entire team. The method depends upon the player's personality.

Upon occasion, Berenson will raise his voice, but never without reason. While some coaches may yell just to get something off their chests, Berenson will not indulge himself. He will yell if he thinks it will fire up a team, or if he feels a player needs a dose of reality. "Our team knows that I will be quick to jump on [them] if I think the team is slipping in terms of work ethic."

Berenson is particularly patient with his younger players, especially the freshmen. He is forgiving of mistakes and quick with words of encouragement. But by the time the player is an upperclassman, Berenson raises his level of expectations. He demands his older players to play the game they way they have been taught and to cover for the mistakes the younger players may make. In this way, the players coalesce as a team and the older players learn valuable leadership skills.

Recognition

Berenson looks for players who, as he says, "want the challenge. They want to try and climb the mountain. They want to try and be the best.

They want to be a big fish in a big pond." Berenson wants his players to think big and when they achieve their goals, he is happy for them. Star players at Michigan receive plenty of attention from fans and media.

But Berenson knows that hockey is a game that calls for consistent and dedicated play from what he calls role players. "They know what those roles are and they take pride in those roles. It may seem like a limited role to a fan or to a parent; but the player knows that [he has] an important role." That self-knowledge Berenson believes enables the unsung player to receive the recognition he deserves.

Role players are essential to the success of any team. "You have to actually talk to the role players more than you do to stars," says assistant Pearson. "So you spend a lot more of your time actually dealing with those players and trying to make them feel important and Red does a nice job of that."

Says Powers, "[Red] will talk about all the good things [the player] is doing. And then he will sneak in, 'and the goals are going to come. You are going to score a couple goals this weekend.'" As Power says, "You can almost see the kid get an extra zip" from Berenson's encouragement."

Training Future Leaders

Red pushes his assistants as much as he does his players. As a former assistant coach, he understands the limitations of the traditional roles; he looks for men he can learn from. So in addition to wanting an assistant who knows the game, is loyal, and is of good character, Red wants one more thing—"I want them to be capable of taking my job."

And Berenson is determined to give his assistants plenty of hands-on experience. "I have included them in all of our decision making in terms of personnel, line-ups, combinations, lines of defense and power play and penalty killing. They are totally hands-on with this team, and I feel good about that. This is a team effort from the coaches. It is not a one-man effort....This is really three-man coaching."

Furthermore, Red trusts both of his assistants with managing the pipeline for future talent—recruiting. While Red is a man who seems uncomfortable when people say good things about him, he is by contrast, voluble when speaking of his assistants. He credits the more veteran coach, Mel Pearson, for his skill at breaking down the strengths and weaknesses of the opponent. And as well as being a good recruiter, Mel "is very good on the ice tactically, and yet he can still see the team issues from a head coach's perspective."

Of the player turned assistant coach, Billy Powers, Red says, "Billy is a great problem solver. He can take a fragile kid and a fragile problem and handle it better than any of us. He has a real nice, softhearted, sincere way about him. He is great."

As a long-time assistant, Pearson credits Berenson with helping him become a better coach by delegating decision-making. "He has let me develop myself as a coach and a person. At times [if] he feels that maybe I am going the wrong way, he will pull me in and say, 'Well, gee, Mel, I think that you have the right idea, but maybe that is not quite the way to go about it.' He has spent a lot of time with us [assistants], letting us get our feet wet." But he is "always there when we fall, to pick us back up and push us on our way."

For his part, Powers says, "We know who the leader is, but he makes us feel as if our every decision is just as important as his. I think that is a special quality." Berenson's delegation to his coaches has evolved over time, in part because of his confidence in their abilities as well as what he calls his own "maturity as a coach." Red is direct about what he receives in return from his coaches. "I learn things from them every day."

Leader as Learner and Teacher

Berenson is blunt about the coaching process. "You don't start at the top. You learn from your own mistakes and you learn from watching your players. You have to patient, you have to be persistent, you have to have confidence in yourself, you have to believe in yourself and want to do this."

Most importantly, Berenson believes a new head coach must be "open to learning. I have learned about coaching and a lot more about the game since I retired as a player. The easiest part is to play. The more difficult is to teach it, direct it, and of course, coach it." Furthermore, Berenson emphasizes consistency. "If it is important on Monday, it has to be important on Friday as well. The players have to understand what the expectations are and it can't change dramatically from day to day."

Putting Together a Team

Coaches, according to Berenson, are responsible for assembling the team. It is a job not without pitfalls. After all, programs like Michigan's recruit star players. The challenge for the coach is to blend their shining talents with all the other shining talents on the team to create a tight, cohesive unit. "We really need to teach them and encourage them to learn how to play and think like a team player. I think from day one we will continue to make examples of team [issues]." For this reason, Berenson makes a habit of emphasizing team achievements over individual goals.

When speaking of teamwork, Berenson can draw upon the example of a consummate team player, Brendan Morrison. When Michigan won its NCAA title in 1996, Morrison hugged the NCAA trophy and said, "This is for all the players who played at Michigan and never won a championship. This is for you guys!" Red is incredibly proud of that moment. "You talk about the ultimate team player; not only thinking of the team, but thinking of the program and the history of the program. I just thought it was the greatest thing he could have said."

It also was a moment that encapsulated what Michigan was all about—honor, tradition, and teamwork. When former players saw Morrison on television, many wrote to Berenson saying, "they just felt like they were right there with the team." They all sensed that this wasn't just another hockey game that Michigan won. This was something special."

Reflection as Growth: Getting Over Tough Losses

Losses are part of the playing process. One of the toughest for Berenson was a loss to University of Maine in triple overtime in the semi-finals of the NCAA tournament. The game lasted an exhausting 100 minutes. In his comments to the team after the game, he was generous, "We didn't lose the game; we just didn't win the game. You know, we played as well as we could play."

Tough losses strengthen the character of the team and, according to Berenson, also provide a learning experience. "You have to take the positives out of a [loss]. Then you have to say, 'What was missing?' Is there anything we could do better if we had to play that game over again? Is there anybody in this room who thinks they could play better and why and what would they do differently?' Questions like that open the door to learning from mistakes as well as motivation for future games, whether it is the next day, or the next season."

When asked about reflection, Berenson is characteristically down to earth. "Yeah, I call that worrying. I worry a lot. I don't worry about our program. I feel that our program is going in the right direction and I think we have a lot of good people around the program. But I worry about the day-to-day progress, the development, the improvement, the work ethic, the day-to-day on the ice and I think that if you worry about the day-to-day enough then pretty soon the years take care of themselves."

Looking back at the program he has established, Red reflects, "I think the vision is even stronger now than when I came. We have good kids, people who want to come here and excel, people who are committed and have their priorities straight."[4]

Preparing for the Future

Many of the players Michigan recruits have expectations of playing professional hockey. And while Berenson is known for his emphasis on the academic side of college hockey, he knows that some of his players may indeed play professionally. And he wants them prepared. According to Pearson, "Red tries to educate the players that it is not all 'peaches and cream.' Professional hockey players have so much down time that they are not used to having in college. He wants them prepared for that and for how you handle that down time." Specifically, Berenson encourages those professional players to continue to take classes, read, and best of all, invest their money wisely.

On Personal Leadership

Tom Goss, Michigan's athletic director from 1997 to 2000, puts Berenson's leadership into perspective. "Coach Berenson has been a leader at Michigan since he was here as a student. His dedication to values is reflected in the students he recruits and the success of the hockey program. His natural ability to lead has made all the difference in the hockey program since he took over in 1984."

Berenson expects his players to be leaders, too—particularly the captains. "You are an assistant captain because of what you do on the ice," says Bobby Hayes, co-captain of the 1998–99 team, "You have to be the hardest working guy. You've got to set an example for your teammates and that is what leadership is pretty much all about. It is being the guy your teammates can look to for encouragement and motivation."

When asked to regard his own leadership attributes, Berenson is characteristically self-deprecating. "I don't look at myself as a leader per se. I look at myself as a coach. Before I got here, I looked at myself as a player." Coaching, as Berenson says, "is a pretty worthwhile profession. It is having good kids, a good program, good people and doing the right thing."

Coaching Philosophy

Berenson's approach to coaching is as direct as he is. "I think everybody can be better than they think they can be. We all put ceilings on ourselves to the point where we are comfortable and we are not sure that we want to go beyond that. But I try and lift that ceiling for every player."

One true measure of greatness in coaching is how former players regard their coach. For some, Red is a father figure; for others, he is a teacher and they are grateful for the time he invested in them. All, however, respect him for the coach he is. Players credit Berenson with teaching them more about hockey, certainly; but more importantly, most believe Red taught them to be better men.

Put another way, Berenson's leadership style is about turning athletes into believers, in themselves as athletes, students, and men of character. That is the essence of Red Berenson, a coach for the whole player.

JILL KER CONWAY
Leading Forward by Looking Back

Her manner is proper. Her poise is exceptional. Her diction is precise. Just what you might expect from a woman who has spent her life in academia. Her politeness and polish seem from another era, when women supposedly knew their place; that is, when they were to be seen and not heard—at least not much.

You would never know, by looking or even listening, that this former college president spent the first ten years of her life as a youngster on her parent's sheep station in the Australian Outback. It was out there helping her father tend sheep, doing the job of her brothers who were off to school and men who had been called to war, that her leadership characteristics first developed. It was a "world in which you just figured out how to solve problems. Nobody wasted much sympathy on you." The times and land were simply too harsh.

Early Leadership

In the first volume of her memoirs, *The Road from Coorain*, Conway talks of herding sheep. As a youngster her voice was not commanding enough to get the sheep dogs to pay attention to her, but over time she found a way to get them to obey her. Concern for her father's heart condition drove the young Jill to do more and more. "I now found myself volunteering for jobs I was not quite sure I could do, in order to be sure that [my father] had more time to rest....There was no getting around that the work was there and had to be done, and so I fell early into a role that it took me many years to escape, the person in the family who would rise to the occasion, no matter the size of the task." [1]

And it was here in the Outback that she learned three lessons of leadership that helped form her character: self-reliance (there were no experts around); physical courage in the face of danger; military history as a basis for strategy. "The men on the ranch, including my father, were veterans of the 1914–18 War; they relived the battles by drawing battle lines in the dirt."

She also gained another valuable lesson from those veterans. "I learned that it was okay to fight which is often not in a woman's background." It was instruction that would steel her courage and strengthen her ambition. Even though the very young Conway could face the travails of the harsh land, her homeland was not exactly hospitable to women. "I grew up in Australia at a time when women were absolutely cast in the role of housewife and mother. And people who moved outside of that pattern were seen as strange. Particularly strange." Her most poignant example is that of her mother, a trained nurse who surrendered her career to move to the Outback with her father.

Mother's Example

"[Mother] was super competent, and I always feel that many of the things that have helped me live my life I learned from her. She was a superb manager of time, and she gave me the sense that as a child that one could do anything one wanted to do.

"I learned time management, system and order, and forward planning from her...[as] she worked two jobs, bookkeeper by day and nurse by night, in order to afford my brothers' school fees, and eventually, mine.

"So I never for an instance thought that if I married and had a child I wouldn't be able to pursue my career. [Mother] was the cook, the laundress, the baker, the bookkeeper, the gardener, and she taught [her children] school, and yet she always found four hours a day to read." [2]

"There is always time in the busiest life for things you give a high priority to. There is no excuse about saying you don't have time to exercise or no excuse for saying you don't have time to read, which means you are not organizing your time rightly....That might mean getting up at four o'clock, but I learned from [my mother] that you don't have to sleep that much."

Pioneering Leadership Roles

As a schoolgirl, Conway loved the literature of Tudor England, Shakespeare in particular. Her exploration of this literature also led her to her first female leadership role model, Elizabeth I. Even today Conway admires Elizabeth's ability to take command in what was then a patriarchal society.

Despite graduating with first-class honors from University of Sydney, Conway suffered a major disappointment, a turndown for a job by Australia's Department of External Affairs. It was a rejection that benefited her in the long run but in the short run pointed out the perception of women in Australia as second-class citizens. "Now I understood directly and personally what injustice rooted in assumptions of biological superiority meant…It chilled me to realize that there was no way to earn my freedom through merit. It was an appalling prospect." [3]

It was this kind of attitude that compelled Conway to make her way outside of her homeland. It sent her to Harvard where she earned a Ph.D. in history and later a position at the University of Toronto where she became the first woman vice president in the institution's history.

As a female executive subjected to the scrutiny of male peers who did not consider her equal, as well as feminist scholars and students who figured she would be a "soft touch" for their concerns, Conway learned to be her own person. "[As a woman leader] you have to be better prepared than anyone else, and you have to learn to take over a meeting or a group." Preparation is particularly critical if the leader is the one generating the plans that will govern an organization's future.

In 1975 Conway was elected the first female President of Smith College, an influential women's college in Massachusetts. There, she created a management development program to help women in middle management move up the ladder. Furthermore, she developed a program for older women to return to college. And it's working. "We graduated women who are in their sixties—musicians, artists, lawyers, doctors, teachers." [4]

Leadership Lessons

Conway credits her upbringing in a British-style boarding school with shaping her initial ideas on leadership through expectations. "We were an elite. Ergo we were born to be leaders. However, the precise means of leadership was by no means clear." [5] Naturally, hers is a quiet kind of leadership. No raised voices. No heavy hand. Conway leads by setting forth expectations. She sets high standards that others want to follow.

"I think that a woman leader has to be able to signal through body language and tone of voice that she is not a threat to the men around her and that she is on the team. I think that is a hard lesson for women to learn because their training—unless they have played a lot of team sports—doesn't make them automatically fit into a team role. Also, if you are nervous or frightened, it is hard to have a soothing and reassuring voice."

Conway considers listening skills a great asset to leadership. "Sometimes it has gotten me into trouble because people misinterpret [my attention as agreement], but I train myself to pay fairly close attention to any other person, especially in a conflict situation." From listening, leaders can learn to prioritize the issues that matter most to themselves and their constituents. "I had a small staff and I would often run through that list [of priorities] with them. We would argue about which [issues] were winnable and which ones were not."

Conway believes that leaders must learn to husband their resources in order to succeed with the issues that matter most. "At the beginning of every academic year, I would just look at all the issues and figure out which were the ones I had a chance of winning, and which ones just to housekeep because it was not the right time to tackle them [because] I didn't have the backing."

Building trust is an absolute for leadership. Trust does not develop overnight; it must be nurtured through frank and honest discussions. Conway would counsel her staff, " 'Look, there are these things that you are not doing right. I need you to tell me what I'm doing which is making your job more difficult.' Once you have established that kind of rapport, I think that delegation is very easy."

Along with delegation comes recognition. "Sit down with your people. Congratulate them discretely, or in front of others," advises Conway. Such behavior by a leader creates a positive effect on morale that is contagious throughout the entire organization.

Another valuable leadership attribute Conway values is reflection, a powerful tool of self-examination. Reflecting upon experiences from childhood, adolescence and young adulthood can provide insight into an adult's decision-making process. "I think if you understand what some of your internalized reactions to situations are, you can subject them to analysis [to] decide whether they are appropriate or not. Memory is very important in that respect."

Conway would know this better than most. As a memoirist, Conway is in a unique position to evaluate the power of reflection. Telling one's own story is a form of self-examination. The deeper we go into our own life histories the more we can learn about why we are what we are. "It's good to be able to confront reality and deal with painful experiences as real rather than through fiction." [6]

Furthermore, reflection helps put decisions into perspective. "I think instead of trying to convince yourself of the correctness of your opinions by telling them to someone else, you have time to put yourself in the place of the other person or persons. By figuring out the root cause of an argument or disagreement, Conway learned "to be more accommodating to the person who is upset."

Leadership Legacy

Having retired from the presidency of Smith in 1985, Conway's leadership remains vivid in her writings. Her most recent book, *When Memory Speaks,* deals with men and women of history from Dame Julian of Norwich through Ben Franklin, W.E. B. DuBois, and Katharine Graham.

Jill Ker Conway is a leader who uses remembrance of things to gain a better perspective. Hers is a leadership that enriches itself through history as a means of preparation for the future. So part of her legacy will be her gift to young women. Conway believes that leadership can be taught and in her executive roles she took time to coach younger women. She credits her pursuit and love of history with her own leadership abilities. "I wouldn't have been nearly as good at running institutions if I hadn't studied the great medieval institutions and their evolution."

"I think that great leaders have a sense of history. They understand either intuitively or rationally, the contending social forces that they are trying to change. That [lesson] is not taught in any leadership-training program, although it is taught by studying history.

"I always tell the people who work for me, especially the very young ones and the women, to go study military history. Find out what the great generals did and how they managed. [Great military leaders] managed to re-conceptualize the strategic and tactical situation in order to formulate [and execute victory]."

This lesson in history is one that Conway absorbed her at father's knee so many years ago when she sat and watched him and his comrades-in-arms discuss their World War I battles.

Memory, which Conway has nurtured throughout her life, has enabled her to overcome incredible odds first as a young woman and later as a leader making her way in a society that had no time for women in authority. Just as her father toiled against a bleak and unforgiving landscape, so too, has Conway toiled within an unforgiving "human-scape." Both were equally harsh and cruel, but both land and people ultimately bent to the will of a determined father and an equally determined daughter.

This personal history has enabled Conway the historian to become Conway the leader, determined and driven to succeed by following her conviction and her own moral courage.

SKIP LEFAUVE
Leadership of the Whole

Throughout its history, the automotive industry has been shaped by men who seemed larger than the businesses they helped establish. Henry Ford implemented mass-manufacturing. Alfred Sloan built the modern corporation. Eliji Toyoda created a legacy to quality. And as giants of their time, automotive executives ruled with the impunity of royalty and the might of generals; on their decisions rode the fate of millions of vehicles and billions of dollars.

Yet how many of these executives ever served as father of the bride to a dealership employee at a customer loyalty reunion held at a factory? Not one that I know of.

That's one distinction that Richard "Skip" LeFauve can claim, among many others. In contrast to automotive titans of the past, LeFauve, who served as president of Saturn Corporation for more than a decade, is a different breed.

Big Picture Leadership

LeFauve is a leader who considers himself part of a larger picture—part of the "whole." According to LeFauve, "A leader immediately recognizes where the interdependencies exist and how they can be played in a positive way in order to help solve issues related to the whole. A lot of people never quite grasp the whole. They always want to focus in on a little piece and never recognize the interdependency factor."

"There is a tendency for leaders to focus on the part of the business they grew up in. They are expert there and they tend to dive very deep into that subject and kill it. You never want to work for a guy who is an expert in your subject, because they will beat you to death. The generalist may not know a lot about your business, but he will ask the important questions." And it's by asking questions and finding solutions that LeFauve believes a leader helps the entire organization—the whole—grow and prosper.

Where did LeFauve first learn leadership? As a young engineer in a General Motors factory, LeFauve became the point man. "You become the leader of that network because they look to you for the coordination and communication among the network. So, you become an informal leader. You don't have any formal title as leader. But you're the one who knows what the whole is."

LeFauve is a true believer in consultation, cooperation, and commitment. When he was president of Saturn, one reporter wondered if he were "an automobile executive or a general in the Salvation Army."[1] Under his leadership, Saturn moved from a concept to a full-production company.

LeFauve's leadership style is uniquely personal. He knows organizations begin and end with people. It is in this humanity that a leader must step away to size up the entire picture. "I think that's what leadership is—getting out of your tunnel, getting out of your chimney or silo. The leader who has a sense of what the wholeness is can help individuals in their silos better understand the whole."

In the process LeFauve helped shepherd one of the most intriguing labor-management partnerships of the 20th century. LeFauve once said, "Saturn is more than a car. It's an idea. It's a whole new way of doing things, of working with our customers and with one another. It's more of a cultural revolution than a product revolution."[2]

Leadership With Vision

According to Michael Bennett, former president of the United Auto Workers local representing Saturn, "Skip had a vision and was always able to articulate what Saturn was meant to be." While Saturn has it roots as a dream of Roger Smith, the former chairman of General Motors, it was LeFauve, together with his team of management and union people, who brought it to fruition.

Dora Mack, one of the original 99 members of the Saturn start-up team, credits LeFauve with embracing the idea of partnership that "radiated throughout the organization." Bennett credits LeFauve with helping to make Saturn the epitome of management and labor working together. The secret of Saturn is worker commitment. Workers share in the decision-making process, including selection of retailers, work design, and fellow workers. Their goal is very focused: to build an affordable, world-class, high-quality, small car.

Much of Saturn's success can be attributed to LeFauve. "He was the fundamental architect of what Saturn would be. He was very visionary," states Bennett. Mack says, "We called him Mr. Saturn. Our culture fit him, his personality. He treated us as his most important asset."

Empowered Leadership

At Saturn, executives and union representatives shadow each other; each has input into the decision-making process. As LeFauve explains, "Management might know the market and business as a whole," but they had little knowledge about the needs of the people in the plant who were making the products.

By contrast, the union understood their own people and could anticipate how they would react to management decisions. Therefore, according to LeFauve, the union was willing to work with management to ensure cooperation as well as input into the decision-making process.

LeFauve's appreciation for union involvement in decision-making comes from his family background. His brother was a union representative for a railroad union. Bennett recalls that LeFauve "would listen to the conversations at the family table about labor-management problems...and think there must be a better way" to deal with issues than as adversaries.

During a visit to Saturn by then-Vice President Al Gore, place names for Bennett and LeFauve became switched. Observers recall that Gore remarked that he could not detect any difference in point of view between the union leader and Saturn president. High praise indeed for union-management partnerships. Bennett credits LeFauve with being a good listener who is open to different points of view. Then when he makes a decision, he lives it. Regarding commitment, says Bennett, "He's as sound as a rock."

For LeFauve, leadership must be grounded in firmly held principles. His experience at Saturn demonstrated the importance of this view. "Learning to share the leadership with traditional adversaries was a big challenge. It was such a high risk, such a perceived high risk, that turned out to be almost minimal because it was so successful."

Leadership for the Customer

Commitment to quality is a Saturn priority. Alec Bedricky recalls when GM management wanted to increase volume, LeFauve would not do it until the quality of the vehicle was right. This principle was put to the test shortly after the launch of the first Saturn cars. It was during the time when, according to LeFauve, "you are building reputation." An alkaline problem with coolant was eroding the engines of Saturn cars. Over 1,800 cars would have to be recalled. Not only was the situation disastrous for the cars, it was even more potentially disastrous for the fledgling Saturn enterprise, particularly one that was trying to establish itself as a paragon of quality.

After a two-week period of gathering data to isolate the engine problem, the decision to make the recall was made in twenty minutes. At the time, LeFauve recalls, "we made the right decision for the customer, even though it may cost us our jobs or it may have ended up costing us the company, but we could at least say we did the right thing. And it turned out to be the right thing because people recognized it for what it was." In fact, the fallout from the recall decision was so positive, Saturn was accused of staging a public relations event, something that LeFauve today finds amusing. During the recall LeFauve exhibited the courage to stand fast and do what's right for the customer. That behavior endeared him to his subordinates. He was "walking the talk" and they admired him for it.

In the process, Saturn has become what brand management expert David Aakers calls a "charismatic brand," inspiring the same kind of loyalty as the buyers of Apple Computer, Harley-Davidson, and yes that automotive icon from an earlier age—the original Volkswagen Beetle.[3]

The relationship that Saturn manifests with customers is a reflection of the relationship that exists within Saturn Corporation. Many companies pay lip service to knowing the customer; at Saturn, knowing the customer took a personal turn. "We had [Saturn employees] actually go out and sell cars. We encouraged them to go into the dealers and retailers stores and meet people. We had them sit in on the customer contact line where people would call in with a problem. [We wanted them] to be there to actually hear the person's frustration…so they could quickly identify with the customer."

In a way, LeFauve's relationship with Saturn was all part of the continuing education of a young engineer turned grand old man of employee empowerment. "If you want to learn the essence of leadership, become an engineer," writes LeFauve in a revealing article. "Then attempt to develop a new product or redesign a key work process, and see how far you get on your own."[4]

Letting Others Speak First

"Leaders" continues LeFauve, "get results only through the committed efforts of others." Leadership for LeFauve begins with letting others speak first. "The leader should never put their opinion in first." For LeFauve, holding back from speaking first is a matter of self-control.

"You always want to bring out the opinions or the data from all members of the team. You identify who the stakeholders are, and be sure those stakeholders are represented in your decision process....This leads to consensus, a key component of organizational harmony. "You encourage consensus by your patience. If you are a leader in the formal sense and you immediately jump to a decision based on initial input and then go into a sell mode, you are a salesman and not a leader."

Leadership must be grounded firmly in two-way communications. LeFauve believes that everyone within the organization needs to communicate to one another. "If you can't do it yourself, be sure that somebody else is doing it. That is a discipline." The globalization of business puts unique demands on communications, in part because you surrender the "luxury" of gathering key decision-makers for a quick meeting. But communications are an imperative. "You must stay in contact."

Leadership and Coaching

LeFauve believes that employees need to know the organization cares about them as individuals. "If you've got a leader who doesn't care about people, he may get short-term results, but not long-term results." If the care element is missing, believes LeFauve, employees catch on quickly and will do only what is necessary to get by. If they sense a commitment from their leaders, they will be willing to exert extraordinary effort.

The way leaders demonstrate caring is by being available, walking the floor. In this way, leaders learn who their employees are as individuals. Caring for others is a leadership attribute that LeFauve values above all others. And it is how he would like to be remembered. "As somebody who cared. Just that simple."

Caring requires nurturing, which can be accomplished with coaching. "[Coaching] is individual encouragement." LeFauve draws an analogy between coaching sports and leadership. "A coach doesn't actually play the game, but he is there to select the players and help them hone their skills. That is really what a leader does."

According to Jim Farmer, who served as public relations director for Saturn, "Skip was constantly referred to as the coach. In that he knew the game, he coaches his players to perform their best. He taught us that leaders have to teach....Skip was not running [an organization], he was coaching a team....We were focused on winning and serving the customer."

"Skip is a teacher," states Alec Bedricky, who served as director of Quality and Purchasing at Saturn during Skip's tenure. During his seminar sessions with management and union leaders, LeFauve would demonstrate "how to be high performance leaders. He integrated people, technology, and business in a way that enabled [employees] to become successful." In LeFauve's leadership style, more can be gained from sharing than preaching. For these reason, Bedricky remembers, "He never talked down to people. He always talked with people."

LeFauve is careful to delineate leadership responsibilities. "You can't be a coach all the time. Sometimes you've got to be the boss. And it is the leader's responsibility to define whether or not to be the boss or the coach, or to be the teacher."

As a leader committed to helping his people learn, LeFauve believes it is necessary to take time to celebrate the wins. Furthermore, it is important to recognize individuals who have done a good job. And to do it in public where they can receive the admiration of their peer group. "Criticize in private and praise in public. It's nothing new, but it is really important."

On Reflection

LeFauve believes that a leader's greatest challenge is finding time to think. He has a simple solution to make it happen. "Schedule it. Put it in your calendar." LeFauve will go so far as to put thinking topics on his "to do" list. By scheduling reflection time as he would an event, LeFauve disciplines himself to think about important issues. Furthermore, the scheduling process encourages ruminative thinking; that is, the pondering of issues and questions over time.

In addition, LeFauve likes to make think-time a dialogue with a trusted associate. "It is a good idea if you can have somebody thinking with you, too." LeFauve believes such a technique helps him with nagging issues that require an outside perspective. Just talking it out with another person helps him shed new light on the problem.

Teaching Leadership

Upon leaving Saturn and the Small Car Division, LeFauve headed up General Motors University. His challenge was to take what he had learned at Saturn and disseminate it throughout all of General Motors. "The charter [of GMU] is to provide the education and training needs of the people at General Motors" in accordance with the business plan. In this way, LeFauve married his knowledge of business with his understanding of people in a way that has enabled GM leadership to teach its business principles to employees throughout the corporation.

While LeFauve retired from General Motors at the end of 1998, his legacy continues at Saturn as well as throughout GM as a whole. According to LeFauve, leaders are everywhere; they simply need the opportunity to exert themselves. The challenge for organizations is to create an environment where people can lead. LeFauve's own personal leadership continues. He remains active as a director on corporate boards, including Harley-Davidson. And his interest in education remains strong; he serves on the board of the Panasonic Foundation, which works with public school systems.

And when you think about it, much of LeFauve's career has been about creating opportunities for others. UAW's Michael Bennett credits LeFauve with teaching him how to be a better leader. "Skip is one of the finest people to be around and to learn from." LeFauve's legacy will be his commitment to individuals, as a man and as a leader. He founded his leadership style on the principles of people first, corporate rules second. And by doing so, LeFauve realized, as enlightened leaders do, that the organization will do even better because it will have the support and commitment of the individual. When that concept takes hold, anything is possible.

JANETTE JACKSON
Leadership in School

It has been said that you can judge the quality of a leader by walking through the environment in which she lives. If this is the case, then Janette Jackson is doing one heck of a job. She's the principal of Allen School, an elementary school in Ann Arbor, Michigan, where the halls are clean and wide and decorated in lively colors and with messages about, by, and for children.

The cheerful look of the halls is mirrored in the sunny disposition of Jackson, a dozen-year veteran of school administration. In a field that is subject to burnout and cynicism, Jackson is relentlessly optimistic, searching for the brighter side. For someone charged with the lives of children, it is an outlook to be admired.

Her approach to education is founded in a question related to children's outcome: "What do we want [our children] to be, look like, act like, and contribute to the world?" That query forms the basis of her vision of education as well as her leadership role.

This vision is evident in what Kathy Macdonald, whose two children attended Allen School, labels as Jackson's leadership "cues," specifically her "use of language." Jackson communicates her concern for students by phrasing issues in terms of what the student needs rather than what the administration requires.

Doreen Poupard, a recently retired assistant superintendent, says Jackson's leadership style is rooted in her competence in children's education as well as her "moral responsibility for children." Jackson is an educator who uses data to get a picture of a situation, then uses her people skills to create a genuine learning community where teachers and children alike can grow and learn together. Very importantly, Poupard says that Jackson is sincere in what she does. "Kids can see she truly does care about them."

Jackson's approach is refreshing and in some ways, novel: in order to foster a positive educational experience for her students, she addresses children by addressing the educational needs of her teachers. "We are developing a learning community and we can't do that in isolation. We can't just expect that students are going to be learners, if we are not [so] as adults." For this reason, Jackson has created the new staff position of "facilitator for team learning"—an individual responsible for helping teachers learn.

It's an idea whose time has come. Jackson believes, "In no other successful corporation or business, do people approach their craft in isolation the way teachers do." Jackson is determined to tear down those walls separating the educational community from the "outside world." Embracing ideals of organizational learning, which stress personal mastery, team development, and logical problem-solving, Jackson and her staff continually formulate new ways to help teachers learn.

The staff facilitator fosters a learning community in several ways. First, she fills in as on-site substitute teacher to allow the regular teacher to take classes. Second, she co-teaches particular lessons to help the teacher either learn new material, or bring fresh new ideas to the classroom. Third, she works as a mentor to younger teachers, working with them as a one-to-one coach to help them sharpen their teaching skills.

Nan Gill, a former elementary principal turned educational consultant, says that Jackson "really understands that the structure you create will generate the behavior you get." Gill credits Jackson with developing schedules that enable teachers to share their experiences, learn by team teaching, and establish common time for teacher planning. Fostering a learning community lies at the root of Jackson's leadership style because it gets to who she is as an individual.

On the Challenge of Being Principal

Jackson regards principalship as a matter of "getting all of the staff and all of the community to buy into the notion that when we teach, we are really investing in the future." She believes it is her responsibility to allow kids to practice the skills they need to be successful adults. She itemizes these skills as critical thinking, problem-solving, proficiency in math, reading, and science, as well as compassion. "If they don't get a lot of practice with that now, it is going to have a negative impact on us as a culture."

Jackson is forthright about her commitment. "It isn't enough for us to say, 'Well, we have done our job.'" Instead Jackson believes schools must ask themselves: "Have we pushed kids to the limit?" in terms of expectations. By setting high expectations for achievement, then the "challenge is to keep everybody moving up."

Beverly Ingraham, the team learning coordinator, says Jackson is "organized with a purpose. She reminds us of our goals all the time. She can see end results, and she keeps the children in mind. We achieve for the children."

Define Your Crisis

As principal, Jackson has many demands on her time. Over the years, she has learned to prioritize. "We have a saying around here, 'Define your crisis,' because I think that one person's crisis isn't another's. And I think sometimes we stop ourselves from doing our best job because we get caught up in the minutiae and the urgent, but not important, stuff which really pulls us away from our real mission and our real work in life."

"So unless there are flames or gushing blood, I have to stop and say, 'Is this really a crisis or is it a problem, or is it something that needs a long-term solution?' Together we will get there, but rarely do I find that I have to stop everything I am doing unless a student is in need."

Jackson keeps her priorities focused in the time she spends in staff meetings. "We try very hard to save our staff meetings for learning together, or for discussion and decision making of import and relevance to the instructional program." Discussion of scheduling and other minutiae are handled off line.

Demonstrate Leadership

Jackson is clear about demonstrating leadership. "If I say I am going to do something, I do it. If I say it is important for us to all teach the curriculum and I am going to hold you accountable for it, then I do that."

"She doesn't ask us to do anything she wouldn't do herself. Her greatest strength is she models what she expects of others," says Ingraham, asserting a claim that is common among those who know Jackson. "Her level of enthusiasm is almost the same as when she began teaching," says Ingraham, recalling that Jackson has been teaching for over twenty-five years. Furthermore, Ingraham says, "She does do her homework. She reads and follows the research. She attends workshops to keep current."

Very importantly, Jackson holds her accountable. "We are here to do what is right for children." That statement serves as her guide toward making the right decisions.

On Communications

Like all effective leaders, Jackson places importance on communication. She does it by what she calls "making connections." Just as the elementary school curriculum draws connections between reading, math, and science, Jackson strives to illustrate how issues affecting staff are connected to the needs of the students and their parents.

Jackson uses the sense of "connectedness" to communicate the big picture. "I think we are so good at analyzing all the parts but we get lost sometimes in the events or the separate kinds of activities that we do. So I find my responsibility as an instructional leader is really to pull people together and again demonstrate the connections."

Furthermore, Jackson uses questions as a means of checking for understanding; she calls it "double-checking." Jackson does more than check for comprehension; she wants to make certain that everyone understands the issues. At the same time, Jackson is open to input from the staff. Communications must be two-way. Jackson works at clarifying issues "so that people will feel more comfortable asking me, 'What did you mean when you said that?'"

The same openness extends to parents. "Janette is accessible," says Macdonald, a management consultant and former teacher. "With Janette, you would forever bump into her the hallway" rather than behind her desk. Furthermore, Jackson "has an incredible facility for the names of both parents and kids." And, adds Macdonald, "she uses them regularly" as a way of making certain that everyone feels a part of the school process.

Macdonald admits that it can be "intimidating" for some parents to make an appointment with a principal. By contrast, Jackson welcomes parental involvement, and is very open to parental input. While she cannot implement every parental suggestion, she does make it a habit to listen to concerns, and make changes when necessary.

Jackson does her best to keep parents informed. Every two weeks she sends a letter home to every parent letting him or her know what's going on at the school. Furthermore, Jackson is a perennial presence at all school events; from first-grade plays to fifth-grade musicals, and all parent-teacher meetings. Macdonald believes that Jackson uses these events as a forum to communicate school news as well as fit the event into the larger picture of what is happening at the school.

On Dissent

Dissent is an issue that can tear organizations apart. Within a school setting dissent can occur among staff and parents, or between teacher and pupils. As ugly as dissension can be, Jackson learned early not to fear it. "First of all I try very hard not to fix it. Not to immediately say, 'Oh, I have the answer.'" The answer may be evident, but Jackson would prefer that individuals come to a solution themselves rather than have it imposed.

"Sometimes the best thing to do is to step back for a day and then to say, 'What do I really know about the issue or what do I need to know?' Sometimes it is best to get a facilitator to come in and help people sort it out. Sometimes I will assume that role if people need to clarify their thinking. But keeping the dialogue going is critical."

Jackson continues, "One of the beliefs I have that comes out of organizational learning is that there is no blame, but there is a sense that people need to take responsibility for their actions and that dissent isn't bad. In fact I think that what I am hopeful for is to have a climate in the adult environment where people can disagree with each other in a respectful, professional way."

With years of teaching and supervising under her belt, Jackson is not "Pollyanna-ish" about resolving all conflicts peacefully. But she does believe that if people can learn to distinguish personalities from issues, dissent can be helpful. "It can promote good change in people, and I think that in the end you build trust. When you dissent, you bond."

On Preparing for Change

Change is endemic within the educational environment. Jackson believes that her job as a leader is to help her staff be proactive "in changes that are beneficial to kids as well as to teachers, and to parents and to the community."

Just as she is a proponent of the learning organization for her staff, she advocates the same principles for her children. "You need to use multiple methods to get kids to think and analyze what they are learning. We must encourage teachers to be on the cutting edge." At the same time, Jackson does not embrace change willy-nilly; "If some trend comes along that isn't going to serve kids, we don't automatically jump on it. First, we analyze and figure out where it belongs in our organization."

On Learning From Your Mistakes

As a new principal, Jackson tried to be very "hands-on" when it came to solving problems and she tells a story about a balky copy machine that was frequently breaking down. Jackson's solution was to have a secretary make copies for everyone. This decision, Jackson later learned, upset the staff because they were accustomed to making their own copies. It was a lesson that taught Jackson that rather than solve problems for others, it is often better to have "others" identify the problem and determine their own solutions. From this example, Jackson learned to stand back to assess a situation before jumping in feet first.

Establishing Expectations

When Jackson joined Allen School, it was a school that ranked near the bottom in terms of test scores. Jackson's task was to turn the school around. So she laid out her expectations to her staff. "I said we are heading down this road that will require us to collaborate, will require us to trust one another, will require a belief in all kids, and will require risk taking and [behavior] modeling."

The staff reaction was not quite what Jackson expected. One by one, the teachers approached her in the days after the meeting to ask if Jackson wanted them to remain. Jackson assured everyone that every teacher was welcome to stay. "But if they chose not to, I would facilitate their move. But if they stayed, they needed to know that I wasn't going to change." Jackson was committed to her child-based value system and was not about to back down.

Macdonald recalls that when Jackson took over, immediately the tone of the school shifted from being concerned about administrative issues to being concerned about student issues. This change is anchored in Jackson's vision for what schools need to be. And it is reflected, Macdonald says, in the way that teachers behaved toward children. Once Jackson took over, teachers responded by emulating Jackson's approach toward children as people to be educated rather than as beings to be mastered.

Assistant supervisor Poupard admires Jackson for her ability to empower her people as well as set high expectations for them. "She's direct, and she's approachable, but you don't mess" with her. Poupard says Jackson "doesn't allow excuses or urgencies to keep her away from the primary mission of learning and teaching."

Gill, a consultant, says that Jackson facilitates and engages her staff in ways that make her vision accessible and personal. Jackson, according to

Gill, has the ability to connect with her teachers because first, they know her vision for the school is rooted in the needs of the children, and second, they are not being asked to do anything she would not do herself. For example, when Jackson first arrived at Allen School, she created time periods where pupils from different grades could come together and learn.

On Problem-Solving

To maximize time, Jackson believes in a systems approach to managing and operating a school. As much as Jackson nurtures an environment of support, she also expects her people to take responsibility for certain issues. Every organization can become bogged down in detail; as a leader, Jackson cannot allow herself to become embroiled in minutiae. As Jackson is fond of saying, "If it is a custodial issue, see the custodian." In other words, go to the source of the problem to find resolution; do not drag unnecessary people into the problem.

If an issue is not resolved, Jackson will become involved to help facilitate resolution. Like all leaders, she does not want to let small problems fester and become larger problems. For this reason, she believes "We need to have routines and procedures so well embedded in the system that you prevent those things from happening and learn from the mistakes that don't occur."

"She's a risk taker," says teacher-facilitator Ingraham. "She's not afraid of controversy." But Ingraham credits Jackson with finding non-confrontational ways to problem-solve. She wants her staff to think and act for themselves. Jackson says, "It is most important for those decisions to get made where they have the impact. I don't want to make decisions for teachers about their classroom." For this reason, Jackson sees her responsibility as providing direction, guidance, and advice when asked.

It also means that Jackson will not ask her teachers to do something she herself would not do. "I model expectations myself. If I am asking them to take risks by co-teaching, then I better be supporting, modeling and facilitating myself."

Jackson believes it is imperative to set forth expectations for her teachers, especially the new ones. "I will do it both ways: individually and oftentimes in teams or groups, just to tell them about this is where I stand and this is what I expect of you. As you have questions, you need to get to me. You have to ask me."

Reflection

According to Jackson, leadership "is sometimes a very lonely job. It is so critical for people to have others they can trust and who have similar responsibilities and understand what it is like." For this reason, Jackson believes reflection is essential and she practices it in two ways. First, she meets regularly with colleagues as well as her supervisors to assess current ideas and practices. She uses these sessions to challenge her own thinking. Second, she makes time to reflect alone. "I do a lot of reading, reflecting and journal writing. I just kind of jot down things as they occur to me...I think it is important to set time aside, whether it is to think, or to read, or to write just for a few minutes can be very refreshing and provide that renewal that we need."

Ingraham says that Jackson also asks her staff to reflect, either in staff meetings or in writing. This method accomplishes two aims; one, it mirrors student behavior; two, it focuses attention on the reflective process.

As her former supervisor, Poupard credits Jackson with an ability to be open to questioning her own ideas. "[Jackson] is totally non-defensive in exploring her own behavior." Poupard says that Jackson welcomes a question that will enable her "to ruminate and explore." While many individuals may feel threatened by open discussion of their leadership, Poupard says Jackson is grounded in a "strong, ethical, moral code" that is rooted in her commitment to children, learning, and education.

Advice to First Time Principals

For Jackson, being a principal is a calling; she was born to it. But at the same time, she is open to sharing her ideas with others. " She's a person people feel very comfortable in calling," says Gill, who was a fellow principal of Jackson's for many years.

When it comes to being a principal for the first time, Jackson is direct. "I would suggest that they do a lot of listening and a lot of asking, not in a threatening way but as a way of seeking information and clarity about what is the procedure, what is the thinking behind it." Her advice is to get "the lay of the land" first by asking open-ended questions in ways that enable staff to tell the new supervisor about the issues, procedures, and personalities of the staff. "Once that is done, the mission is pretty clear."

On Teaching Leadership

As an educator, Jackson is philosophical about whether leadership can be taught. "I am not sure that we can teach leadership in the same way that we might teach somebody how to build a car." She continues, "The psychology of leadership and the skills needed to be a leader can be taught, but I think that the way leadership emerges in people is through opportunity and practice, and a real drive and motivation to be in that role."

It is not an overnight process. "It took me a year to really get a feel." But Jackson is quick to point out that gathering information does not preclude activity. It is important for a leader to set a vision, communicate through example, and live the message. For Jackson it is a matter of leader and staff learning together. But for her, while staff and students change over time, Jackson's personal mission remains constant: "We are committed to learning together and making a difference for kids." Likewise, she believes her staff has a right to expect "honesty, hard work, and follow-through. They need to know they can count on me." Good words for an educator; excellent words to live by for a leader.

DAVID MCKINNON
Relationship-Based Leadership

It had been his company. He had helped to establish and build it, and sold it to a promising bidder. But then the wheels came off the deal. In the space of a few short months, David McKinnon had experienced the nightmare of every successful entrepreneur: creating a business, selling it for a nice sum, and then watching it disintegrate.

McKinnon was not about to give up. He had come too far and owed too many people, not simply money, but his self-respect, to not fight back. So then, with no title and no salary, McKinnon decided to rescue the company he had helped build. He regained control of his company, Molly Maid.

In retrospect, taking control was not difficult, but the task of making Molly Maid viable again was monumental. With two employees from the old business, McKinnon started over. His first task was to address the overwhelming financial obstacles—Molly Maid was over $1.4 million in debt. Fifty-four creditors registered claims of $10,000 or more. McKinnon recalls, "We had to face just about every obstacle you can imagine. We had no capital, no credibility, and no cash flow. We had to make a turnaround very quickly."

Compounding the comeback effort were problems with franchisees, including a lawsuit from some disgruntled ones. Some franchisees thought McKinnon had abandoned them. They were bitter. "Their perception," admits McKinnon, "was that we had walked away with bag loads of money, which wasn't true."

In fact, McKinnon had built the business one franchise at a time to 120. When he decided to sell his stake in the business to a large conglomerate, McKinnon's plan was to remain as president. Unfortunately, the new corporate owners failed to grasp the intricacies of a home-service business as well as franchising. "They talked about regions instead of people. Things that should have taken two minutes took weeks," recalls McKinnon.[1] Again, an entrepreneur's nightmare.

Bottom line, the new owners were not successful in operating a home-service business that was founded on personal relationships, first between customer and franchisee and ultimately between franchisee and management. McKinnon resigned. Soon, Molly Maid floundered—sales plummeted, and some franchisees stopped paying royalties. For McKinnon, the value of his stock evaporated. Having invested everything in Molly Maid, McKinnon was in a precarious financial position and nearly bankrupt—as was Molly Maid. It was then that McKinnon decided he had to take charge.

McKinnon had to persuade the operators that he was not going to sell the business again and leave them hanging without sound management. Put another way, McKinnon was between a rock and hard place with only the force of his vision and the network of relationships he had helped knit together. There was one more asset—his ability to communicate simply and directly to save the company. McKinnon's powers of persuasion, which were anchored within his personal style and credibility, won out. "I was able to convince forty-seven of them to stick with it. I attribute 90% of Molly Maid's success today to those forty-seven people." And it's paid off. The lawsuit was eventually resolved.

Today Molly Maid is a leading home-services company with more than 530 Molly Maid franchises worldwide and annual revenues topping $100 million. McKinnon is CEO and chairman.

Like Boss, Like Company

As much as an organization can be a reflection of its leader Molly Maid is such a company. "Good morning, Molly Maid" says the receptionist. The voice is bright and cheerful, and yes, sincere. Walking through the hallways, you find the same sense of good cheer. Employees greet visitors with a smile and a firm handshake. They make eye contact.

Cynics might assume the friendliness is an act until they meet David McKinnon in person. "David really cares about relationships and that shows in every aspect of his life, not only with his own family and his friends," says Linda Burzynski, President of Molly Maid. "From the very first time he meets someone, he wants to know more about them and make them feel welcome."

Long-time Molly Maid operator Steve Chaput of Upland, California, believes that McKinnon's "most important leadership quality is his honesty and integrity. I've always looked up to David from the first time I met him at a franchise show. He seemed genuine. Knowing him for eleven years has only reinforced my trust and belief in him."

Laying a Foundation for Character and Vision

McKinnon's friendly approach to others likely stems from his upbringing in the Caribbean where his parents were missionaries. From his parents, he gained a commitment to a faith that shapes him. "Character is the one thing that stands the test of time. I think that a leader without character—no matter what the results are—will never be considered a good leader."

Furthermore, McKinnon had good mentors. He credits his first boss with demonstrating to him that character extends to the business world; it was the personal attention that McKinnon remembers best. "He treated me equal to vice presidents." As a fresh-faced kid out of college, that personal attention meant a great deal and it is something McKinnon is intent on passing on to the next generation.

His first bosses saw in McKinnon an ability to look ahead, a key quality if you intend to build businesses. Leaving the corporate world, McKinnon bought a ServiceMaster franchise and made it one of the world's largest. Upon selling his stake in that franchise in 1984, McKinnon and a partner bought the U.S. rights for Molly Maid from the Canadian-based operation. Having been an franchisee, McKinnon understood what it took to attract and retain good operators, men and women willing to make an investment in a business they could run as their own.

Ana Alonso, a Molly Maid franchise owner in Houston, says, "David is a great leader because he has a clear vision of what he wants and has been able to communicate it." For example, McKinnon believes that Molly Maid, operating as it does in the home service arena, is a solid bet for the future. "Molly Maid's success," says Alonso, "is providing professional maid service. And as long as we hold to the 'vision of the professional,' our system will be a success a long time into the future."

Putting Relationships Ahead of Business

McKinnon is a businessperson who puts relationships first; even if it goes against the advice of his attorneys. An example was a rewriting of the franchise agreement to address the concerns of long-time operators. "We will put the relationship ahead of a contract. Doing what's right has nothing to do with contracts."

Principles are priority with McKinnon, says Linda Burzynski. "David is always very conscious of wanting to do the right thing, and I have seen him make many decisions that may not have been the best thing for the bottom line. But, in the long run, David's philosophy is that it really doesn't matter as long as you are doing the right thing, then the business will take care of itself."

McKinnon insists his approach is good for business. "Once people start to understand that this is a real principle inside of this company, people quit looking at their agreements and they start talking. To me that is a very, very positive thing. If we have a problem, an unhappy franchise owner, an unhappy employee, I don't care what the agreement says, we have got to find out why, and what we can do to fix it."

Dealing with franchisees, entrepreneurs like himself, is a tricky business. He knows that franchisees do not want to be told what to do; yet, they crave the operational structure that a franchise organization can provide. McKinnon's solution is to be available as needed. He gives advice when asked; makes suggestions if necessary; but in general maintains a hands-off approach toward an operator's business. In other words, as Burzynski says, "David empowers people with the skills that they need, and then walks away to let them get the job done."

Results-Oriented Leadership

According to McKinnon, "consensus is a big word inside of our organization. It is just part of the culture of our organization that says we are not always going to agree, and we don't." For McKinnon it is important to form a consensus, then leave the room united.

McKinnon believes in results-oriented leadership. "I consider myself very relationship oriented. But, I also expect results and when someone says ', I will produce this number or I will produce this deadline,' I expect it to be done. I think when you get everyone understanding what you expect, over time you can start producing results on an organization wide basis. Then, all of sudden, people start saying, 'Wow, we are getting things done and we have a good leader.'"

McKinnon continues, "My style of leadership doesn't show up until after a while. I believe that leadership is demonstrated, not stated. From what I have seen in business leaders, the successful ones are the strong, quiet types. They are usually not the ones in front of the camera, the ones seeking attention. They are the ones seeking results. And, results take a while to achieve."

For McKinnon, leadership requires an ability to make decisions based upon solid information, and that requires effective communications. "I want the one-minute version of everything. I don't want the gory details. I want to know what the problem is, what impact it has on the organization, and what two or three things someone thinks we can do to fix it."

This sense of responsibility fosters employee loyalty. "My job is to facilitate an environment where people love coming to work, and know what their jobs are." Furthermore, McKinnon adds, "we want happy, profitable, growing franchise owners. That is the job description of everyone on our franchise support team."

Dean Mitchell, a Molly Maid owner in Williamsburg, Virginia, credits McKinnon with the ability to make his views understandable. "If he really believes [in an issue], he makes the point known, although he tries to remain open." Mitchell recalls that McKinnon had strong ideas about the need for Molly Maid service people to wear uniforms as a means of conveying a professional image. According to Mitchell, "McKinnon let it be known, we're still going to have this image. And we went with it."

"If we have an unprofitable franchisee," says McKinnon, "someone is not doing their job. And, if I have a franchisee that is not growing, someone is not doing his or her job. To me it is really just that simple." With that kind of attitude it is no wonder that Molly Maid is one of the nation's fastest-growing franchise businesses.

McKinnon emphasizes communications, but willingly acknowledges his own shortcomings. "Communications is probably the most difficult thing in leadership because my personal style is one-on-one, eyeball to eyeball. But, in a centralized organization like a franchise company, where you have franchises all over the world, your eyeball-to-eyeball times are few and far between. So, I try to do it by passing on philosophies, cultures, through our management team, and it is a slow process. But, I think it does stand the test of time."

Letting Go to Move Forward

The greatest challenge for many self-made business people, after they have launched a business, is to step back and let someone else run it. McKinnon jokes "the more golf I can play, the better job I think that I am doing." In reality, he is only partly jesting. "Unlike a lot of entrepreneurs, I do not treasure office time. A 65-hour workweek is a sign of a poor organization. I believe that you can do everything that a growing, thriving, competitive enterprise has to do in a 40-to-50-hour workweek. Over a year period, if you can't do that, you are probably either short staffed or you have a weak member of the team."

McKinnon follows the advice that General George C. Marshall once gave Dwight Eisenhower: "I must have assistants who will solve their own problems and tell me later what they have done." Many high-profile entrepreneurs have lost their companies by a failure to delegate work and responsibilities to others. Not McKinnon. "I am not a good manager per se. I don't like detail. As your business becomes larger and larger, the job of the entrepreneur is to step back from the day to day management."

For this reason, leadership development is critical to McKinnon. "I think, inside, everyone wants to be a leader. I do believe that leaders can be created, nurtured. It is almost a "parent role" to say: 'I am going to take these four or five people and develop them as leaders.' As a leader you have an obligation to your organization to develop new leaders."

McKinnon's willingness to move to the sidelines is also made possible by his belief in promoting from within. "One of the biggest challenges in growing an organization is when your organization broadens. I want to take the good people from inside the organization who already know our culture, know our philosophy, and put them in those new jobs. The only way that we can successfully do that is if the good people have made themselves redundant, so that they are able to be moved into these other responsibilities."

It is a standard to which McKinnon holds himself. "If I were hit by the proverbial truck tomorrow, Molly Maid would probably go on because we have identified who we are, where we are, and where we want to be."

Giving Back

As a successful businessperson, McKinnon also feels the need to give back. Running a home-services business that is staffed largely by women, Molly Maid identified a problem. "We found," says McKinnon, "that a very high percentage of our employees have been a subject of domestic violence at some time in the past." Furthermore, his franchisees wanted to become involved. This desire to benefit the community led to the establishment of the Ms. Molly Foundation to help families affected by domestic violence. David's wife, Karen, serves as Chairperson of the Foundation.

The effort involves fundraising and the donations of goods to safe houses located in areas where Molly Maid operates. Molly Maid even invites its customers to participate. Employees solicit disposable goods that can be donated to the safe house. The Ms. Molly Foundation has helped many families and was honored for its commitment at a White House reception in 1997.

Commitment to others extends to his family. McKinnon believes that if a person is spending too much time at work, he is losing something more valuable. "The price you are paying is your family, especially if you have a young, growing family like I do. Yet they are a larger priority than my business success. My job is to make sure that [my children] are given the tools and equipment to be successful, productive individuals on their own. They are my biggest priority."

"In my role," McKinnon philosophizes, echoing his upbringing as well as his commitment to doing the right thing, "I'd rather be remembered as a good parent and a good husband first rather than a good businessman."

A Sense of Trust

Operator Steve Chaput is direct about McKinnon. "David is a real down-to-earth person. He can be a friend on one hand, and a business person whom you can trust on the other." It is not only operators and employees who trust McKinnon. In 1999, McKinnon was elected to the board of directors of the International Franchise Association, the world's oldest and largest franchise association. As a board member, McKinnon will work to promote the business rights and values of more than 30,000 franchisee members throughout the world.

McKinnon takes his corporate and board responsibilities to heart, regularly employing reflection to gauge his place in the world. "As a leader, it is necessary to step back and just think. I am a big music lover. I think that one or two hours a week of just sitting and listening to music and contemplating the previous week, month, year is very, very healthy. But, I try not to dwell on the negatives, or the mistakes that have been made, but rather to dwell on how we can take the organization from where we are now to the next level."

Moving to the "next level" will be a challenge, as it is for any organization. But Molly Maid's future will be aided greatly by David McKinnon's legacy of relationship-centered leadership.

RICK SNYDER
Leader as Teacher

When Rick Snyder was in his early twenties, he was teaching law and accounting to undergraduates. His commitment to teaching remains strong some twenty years later, only now his students are business professionals.

In the intervening years he has served as a partner in a large accounting firm, helped establish one of the nation's leading computer companies, earned in excess of $100 million dollars in stock and compensation, and established a $100-million venture capital firm to fund high-technology companies.

For most people that would be enough. Not for Rick Snyder; he has only just begun. This is characteristic of a man who set down many of his life goals when he was just a teen. A glance at Snyder's resume would seem to indicate a man in a hurry. He received his undergraduate degree at age nineteen; his M.B.A. at twenty; and his law degree at twenty-three—all from the University of Michigan in Ann Arbor.

Engage Snyder in conversation and you find a man of purpose, but also one of patience. His tone is cheerful; his demeanor is open and friendly; and his language alternates between anecdotes, humor, and insight. In short, Rick Snyder has accomplished a great deal, but to hear him speak he has a great deal more to accomplish.

Focus on Goals

Snyder began developing his goals when he was still quite young—just age fifteen! The early focus has benefited him in multiple ways. It has enabled him to pilot his life course with firm direction and to benchmark his progress against chosen milestones. Snyder has a name for his planning process, "the analysis of alternative paths." This approach enables Snyder to keep his mind focused on the end-goal, but his plans flexible enough to accommodate unexpected obstacles or detours that life presents. "I tell people that living life by Plan A is not a good way to live. It's too high stress. In terms of leadership, you have to have a direction to go. You have to have a plan A, but you have to say, 'What is the most likely thing to go wrong here?' And if it does go wrong, I still [have] Plan B."

Snyder's goals have helped him to make the right choices in the face of new challenges that always arise. For example, Snyder never expected to live in South Dakota and work for a computer start-up, but he did. His personal vision provided him the structure to integrate the challenge into his life course and move forward appropriately.

Additionally, reaching for goals has served as an inspiration for Snyder. His conviction is that people like having goals and they enjoy attaining them even more. Leaders, according to Snyder, owe it to their constituents to provide direction. "People like goals" and enjoy being part of something that is in the process of being achieved, built, or established.

Leadership With Vision

When Rick joined Gateway, Inc., it was a 700-person operation located in North Sioux City, South Dakota. When he left it was global industry with 11,000 employees on four continents. Much of the early growth can be attributed to the founder of Gateway, Ted Waitt. Snyder admires Waitt's visionary outlook. Where some in the company would be project-ing sales of a billion, Waitt was thinking of ways to make Gateway a $5-billion dollar company. "He was way ahead in saying where this could go and what it would look like." Very importantly, Waitt had the determi-nation and drive to make things happen as well as the "personality and charisma" to inspire others. "[Waitt] could communicate it in a down-to-earth fashion so you could get other people to believe it and follow."

Waitt as CEO and Snyder as chief operating officer worked as an effective team. Waitt concentrated on what he liked and did best, such as marketing, human resources, and customers. Snyder focused on these issues as well as the operational side of the business. Snyder credits Waitt with understanding how to leverage his time and resources where they could have the most impact. Waitt returns the compliment. "He's a very bright guy and driven at the same time. And he's pretty well-balanced at the same time." [1]

Helping run the start-up, Snyder served as a jack-of-all-trades. With his legal background, he, of course, worked with outside counsel, but he did much more. As he points out, when you are in start-up venture you do everything. By contrast, when the company grows, it is necessary to pull back and focus on only those tasks that require your attention. The role is different; you become a supervisor rather than a doer. If you continue to act as doer, you will fail.

This step has been the downfall of many small businesses. According to Snyder, the biggest leap in management is not moving up the ladder, it's taking the first step as supervisor—delegating assignments, supervising workflow, and working with people.

Digital *vs.* Analog Leadership

Snyder's professional education illustrates his worldview. His M.B.A. emphasizes his clinical business side; his law degree accents his understanding of people. Snyder views the world as both digital and analog. With digital, "there is an answer, it's A or B; on or off." This type of decision-making, says Snyder, "can work successfully in scientific, technical markets where you are not interfacing with people."

The analog side of life is "fuzzy," where there may be no single answer to a given question. And herein lies a conflict, says Snyder. "We have focused so much energy on thinking 'digitally' that one of the major challenges we have in the future is making sure that we train people to think 'analog.' As long as there is more than one of us, this analog thing will not go away and we don't want it to, because that is creativity, that's the fun of life."

Knowing Your People

For Snyder, leaders must know their people as well as their situations. As a senior executive at Gateway, Snyder traveled the globe extensively visiting Gateway facilities. Aside from supervising operational details, Snyder made a point of just visiting with employees. He would ask questions in an effort to gain an truer picture of issues, problems, and solutions.

Bob Spears, a vice president of finance at Gateway, lauds Snyder for his ability to communicate. "I think he has a very unique ability of being able to communicate complex issues to the level of the audience. He is very willing to use anecdotes and analogies [to describe] what was really going on. He did not throw his ego into the way he communicated."

Part of Snyder's communication style was acknowledging the good work of others. "If you are doing things right in large part, you don't worry about recognition for yourself. The goal is to recognize others. If you are doing it right, you are providing a mentor role, helping [people] grow and succeed."

Snyder cites the example of an executive at Gateway who created a work environment where people who worked for him would get recognition in the form of regular promotions. "That is the kind of person you really admire and want to move up because good stuff just sort of happens around him," says Snyder. Part of the way good managers succeed is through recognition. It "creates a bigger environment of success. If you are really doing it right, you are creating this broader structure and environment where people are really flourishing."

Snyder finds a flaw in the management succession program at some technology-driven companies. Technically-competent people are pushed to assume management roles. Just because someone, however, is technically proficient, cautions Snyder, does not mean he or she can assume a supervisory role. Management must be very selective. At Gateway, he candidly admits they worked to find ways to keep good, strong, technically-competent people in positions where they could apply their technical abilities without assuming managerial duties. In these cases, compensation must be commensurate with skill, not supervision.

When Snyder announced his decision to leave Gateway, his decision was felt by many he had touched. Bob Spears recalls, "The stream of people walking in and out to wish him well was quite long." The well-wishers included not simply executive colleagues, but people in all levels of the organization. "They felt connected," as Spears attests. "They felt loyalty and gratitude, and wanted to express that."

Leader as Teacher

After Gateway, Rick founded Avalon Investments, Inc., a venture capital firm. Snyder believes that obtaining venture capital is like "dating" and "getting married." "You have to think about all the years that follow." Getting the capital is the "date." Creating an environment where capital can add value "the marriage."

Snyder sees his role as helping a new venture create value by nurturing its leadership team. With Avalon, Snyder is applying his teaching skills along with his business acumen. "I wouldn't enjoy Avalon very much if it was only writing checks to people. That is not the goal. The goal is to give them financial resources to write the check, but also to give them some value-added business advice by being an active board member."

According to Ken Nisbet, who helps find funding for technological ventures at University of Michigan, "Rick is very good at coming in at an early stage...listening and responding with helpful comments. Basically he teaches life lessons. Great teachers listen first, and that's what Rick does. He doesn't preach."

People are drawn to Snyder because of his accomplishments. "People love success stories," adds Nisbet. Once people meet Snyder they like him even more because of his positive attitude. "Seeing problem areas as opportunities rather than problems" is a Snyder strength, says Nisbet. "He doesn't focus on the problem, he focuses on how we can make it happen. He's always convinced that good things can happen."

One entrepreneur Avalon has invested in is Vic Strecher, CEO of Health Media. "Rick didn't ask what my exit strategy was. He wanted to see what we could build." Snyder was interested in what Health Media, an online health information service, could become. At their first meeting, Snyder plunged right in, by starting to draw an organization chart for Health Media. "He's an advisor-consultant," says Strecher. "He's the kind of person [our business] would be paying for. Instead, he's paying me."

Snyder looks for certain types of entrepreneurs, which he humorously labels as "socially acceptable fanatics." He defines such a "fanatic" as a person of vision and determination. This entrepreneur, according to Snyder, needs the vision to know where he wants to go, and the determination to overcome obstacles to arrive there.

To help these businesses flourish, Snyder takes an active role in their education; part of that education includes teaching decision-making. Snyder believes that entrepreneurs need to consider the "digital" (business) issues along with the "analog"(people) issues. "If you understand where someone else is coming from, then you can get an efficient resolution, or an efficient communication."

Furthermore, Snyder wants to play a role in helping these entrepreneurs grow and launch their businesses. Strecher, a behavioral psychologist by training, calls Snyder "a natural teacher, an expert mentor, a natural facilitator." For example, if a young company is struggling with a major decision, Snyder may invite the group out for dinner. There he will describe the issue, encourage discussion, and outline the next steps. In this way, Snyder facilitates decision-making.

Snyder's commitment to teaching comes from his role models. "Throughout my career," says Snyder, "I have been fortunate in having a number of mentors, or people I have really respected in some fashion." Snyder can tick off people from each stage of his life that have helped him along—professors, partners, and of course, Ted Waitt, the founder of Gateway Computer. "I learned some fabulous things from Ted about being a visionary and about being an entrepreneur that I really respect."

Snyder offers sage advice to would-be entrepreneurs. "People are the key. Technologies come and go, so what you are betting on is a group of people working together." He continues, "Typically people overemphasize the technology and vision aspects of the company. They forget the equally important aspects of marketing the business day to day." Execution of business fundamentals is essential to long-term success. At the same time, Snyder is an investor with the long view. "I don't expect everything to go right. If you manage the problems, the venture can be very successful." [2]

Snyder believes in helping others assume leadership positions because he himself has been helped. Bob Spear credits Snyder with helping a number of people at Gateway assume leadership positions, and today Snyder is doing the same with Avalon, helping entrepreneurs lead their organizations into new ventures. "Teaching is central to the way he manages," says Spear.

Learning From Mistakes

Part of teaching involves learning from mistakes. "I learned this at Gateway," says Snyder, "you never want to hide a problem. The sooner you admit you made a mistake or did something wrong, the sooner you can fix it and get back on the right path. Ignoring problems or issues is quite often what kills a lot of people."

Teaching entrepreneurs motivates Snyder, "When I get up to teach I don't look upon it as standing in front of people telling them they need to learn something. I view a teacher as someone who has more experience and knowledge in a particular field. I have a dialogue and try to share [what I know] as well as learn from the students at the same time." Nisbet concurs, "[Snyder's] strength is as a people person. He's a good listener. By listening, he lets people present their image. [He] adds to it with his teachings rather than telling them what to do. He knows there is more than one path. He's open to it and supportive of it. He reinforces that people are important to him."

According to Rob Cheng, a senior manager who worked with Rick at Gateway, Snyder encourages people to look at situations from the perspective of "the other guy"—be it a supplier, or an employee. By adopting an outside perspective, the individual gains perspective that he can use to gain greater understanding of his own situation as well as that of another interested party.

Snyder also shares the global perspective with his entrepreneurs. "You can't count on being better than the person down the street. You have to worry about the person on the other continent. And you don't even know that they exist, but they are out there. And you are competing with them. With the Internet, with technology, with evolution it may not be evident today, but sooner or later essentially there's pure competition around the world."

Making Time for Self and Family

As one who has spent a good deal of time in the computer industry with its very fast product-development cycles, Snyder believes in the need to "reflect on a real-time basis as you go through things."

"Make sure you save time for your personal life. I worked too much for a number of years." Being a workaholic not only compromises family life, it hinders productivity. "You lose perspective and everything suffers. Your work is not as good. You make yourself miserable in many respects." Outside interests in Snyder's view make for a better worker. "You need some stabilizing factors. You need more than one variable in your life. And so what you find is you work more efficiently." Snyder found ways to live his own words of advice. "Since I have this commitment to family, I would work out arrangements with my wife where I'd work late two nights a week and I would be home for dinner the other nights of the week. So you got your work done." Continuing further in his theme, Snyder says, "The tragedy would be if you didn't nurture [those closest to you] while you were helping other people."

For now, Snyder is very fulfilled in nurturing Avalon as well as doing something more personal-spending time with his family. The decision to return to Michigan was sparked by a need for family time; both he and wife are Michigan natives.

Leadership of the Future

But in time, Snyder is yearning to try a larger classroom—the political arena. Sometime within the next decade, he would like to run for governor or senator from Michigan. Again, his old boss, Ted Waitt says, "That's been his plan since I've met him and he really hasn't deviated from that. I have no reason to doubt that he'll be able to accomplish what he wants to accomplish."[3]

Echoing a theme of many public servants, Snyder says, "I want to give back to people. It is not like I owe a debt, but I think I can give something." Part of what he would bring to the political process is credibility, which he values as a key asset to leadership. "What I value the most is my integrity and honesty. You can find smart people. You can find the answers, but fundamentally, one thing you have that you never want to lose is your integrity and character."

Political office also poses another challenge. "Most good people don't want to mess around with it because they think it is too big of a problem," believes Snyder. "But the problem is not going to get fixed unless you get people who are willing enough to say, 'I am not going to let that stop me.' If you want the best leadership, you should want people who are doing that with the highest and best skill sets. You want to encourage people to go into it."

Nisbet credits Snyder with his desire to help his home state. "He could be doing things far safer and more financially rewarding. He has a community orientation. He wants to help the State of Michigan, and Ann Arbor in particular. The money he has made allows him to take risks...and truly try to help people. He does like to work with people."

In the public arena, Snyder will be able to open his teaching skills to the widest arena possible and do some educating on a grand scale. It is in government that Snyder may find his business skills and his human touch put to their greatest challenge.

========

In the fall of 2000 Rick Snyder announced the formation of Ardesta, a new $100 million venture capital fund dedicated to development of MEMS (micro-electromechanical systems) technologies. Many of these technologies are still in the early development stage, but venture capital funding is needed to bring them to fruition. MEMS is seen by many experts as a next-generation technology that may one day be used in a wide range of industrial, medical and scientific applications. As president of Ardesta, Snyder will play a leadership role in the capitalization as well as the management development of individual companies in which Ardesta invests. Additionally, Snyder hopes to create synergies between the scientific and business communities. "We want to be the glue in the marketplace that brings [scientists and business professionals] together."[4]

WOLVERINE BATTALION
Shaping Leaders of Tomorrow

A generation after the Vietnam War, the U.S. military serves a model of organizational transformation. Military themes are popular in fiction and movies as well as on television. Young people today have a more favorable attitude toward the military. This change illustrates what can happen when an organization emerges from crisis, and comes to a hard realization that whatever it was doing is no longer working. Rather than run and hide, it sought to change, and change mightily it did.

The military transformed itself in response to political pressures from the American people and specifically Congress. Funding was cut; priorities were shifted. The Cold War ended. There was a great victory in Gulf War. More and more, the military was called upon to do peacekeeping and disaster relief. And through it all, the number of missions has increased.

Today the U.S. military is an all-volunteer force. It is color-blind; men of color have risen to the highest ranks. It includes women in key roles. Corporate America is taking a hard look at military leadership. The "lessons learned" exercises that stem from after-action reports have served as a template for business school case studies, and in turn have been adopted by a number of businesses.

The military, of course, is not without its blemishes. The sexual harassment cases remain an ugly scar on the integration of women into military service. Furthermore, the military is waging a constant battle to attract quality recruits. Good economic times do not make the task any easier. But, by and large, the military of the late Nineties is a quantum leap from where it was in the mid-Seventies.

Actually, the military has undergone two dramatic changes: one, rebuilding itself from the ashes of the Vietnam conflict; two, transforming itself into a Post-Cold War fighting force. General Gordon Sullivan, former Army Chief of Staff, together with one of his officers, Michael Harper, have written eloquently of this transformation in their book, Hope is Not a Method. *According to Sullivan and Harper, the way the Army met these challenges was through leadership.*[1]

Military leadership, unlike the leadership in other organizations, serves as a context for the entire organization. The leadership commissioned and noncommissioned officers exert is forged by a system of values, honed by a code of ethics, and reasoned by a system of laws. Over and above this bedrock is the commitment to national service. There is honor in their leadership.

From where does this leadership emerge? The answers are varied as the men and women who serve, but to find out I took a look at the Army Reserve Officer Training Corps (ROTC) program at the University of Michigan. The young men and women of the Wolverine Battalion undergoing training there will be the ones to lead the military into the next century; it is upon their shoulders, and shoulders of thousands of other likeminded young men and women, that our future security rests.

The lessons these recruits learn here at Michigan is something that may be applicable to everyone wishing to learn more about leadership.

Hands-On Leadership

Leadership starts with the commander of the Army ROTC unit, Lieutenant Colonel Christopher H. Lucier. Tall, well-muscled, and quick with a strong handshake, Lucier looks every inch a military person, even his gait signifies purpose. As commander, charged with shaping the hearts and minds of the next generation leaders, he knows he has a big job to do.

It is this professionalism that gives the leadership its context. Here in Army ROTC, leadership is hands-on. "One of the interesting things about ROTC is, as seniors, the cadets actually run the program," says Lucier. "I'm here to provide them with guidance, mentorship, and resources, but there's a cadet battalion commander and executive officer to the cadet staff. They plan the training, they evaluate the training afterwards, and they make adjustments."

Juniors are put into situations where they can perform as leaders of a squad, a platoon, or company commander. Throughout the process, observers comprised of cadets and officers watch and evaluate, looking for performance in delegation, communication, motivation, and other leadership skills. Juniors also evaluate their own performance by asking themselves a series of questions such as: "What did I do this week? How did I do? What were my strengths and weakness? Where did I go right and wrong?"

The cadets of the Wolverine Battalion have a sense of purpose and bearing that extends beyond their years. In class and during field training, they are attentive and purposeful. When you meet them, they make eye contact and present themselves with poise. And when they speak in public, their voices are firm, their diction clear. At the same time, they are every inch college kids, full of spunk and spirit. While the military shapes them with a 200-year plus tradition, they are very much part of today's culture. They, after all, are still the children of MTV.

A graduate of the Wolverine Battalion, First Lieutenant Kenny Kuniyuki says, "The ROTC program enforces a lot of responsibility. Juniors and seniors have very high expectations because they're getting ready to become Army officers." The program emphasizes hands-on leadership. The Army understands that leaders do not come from classrooms; they are made in practice. As Kuniyuki, who became a Tank Platoon Leader with the 1st Cavalry Division, explains, "The seniors are responsible for evaluating the juniors on their leadership skills. At the same time, they look after the freshmen and the sophomores." As such, the seniors become mentors for everyone in the program. Furthermore, "ROTC is unique in terms of leadership because you also get to see the followership aspect. Most of those programs that teach leadership churn out a lot of chiefs who have no idea what it's like to be a follower."

Staff officers like Lucier and his team of commissioned and noncommissioned officers provide further guidance; "Our job is to teach, coach, and mentor" through the task, performance, assessment, and review process. This hands-on training is essential because upon graduation these young cadets will be on active duty and responsible for the lives of the men and women in their command. As young officers, they will be required to lead: that is, plan, delegate, communicate, recognize, and all the other essential tasks for twenty to thirty people in their command. And they will be doing it at an early age—twenty-two years old, on average.

Guidelines for Leadership

The direction of the Michigan Army ROTC program is determined by Lucier's command philosophy—how he and his troops will do business in his outfit. A memo to his troops gives a brief, but direct, four-page overview of his views. Right at the top, the memo states: "My command philosophy is built on four characteristics that I feel make up the foundation of every successful organization: standards, discipline, teamwork, and having fun."

The first three are expected; every group needs standards by which to live and standards by which to challenge themselves. Every successful group needs discipline that comes from adhering to a common goal and common objectives. Likewise, every organization needs the support and cooperation of its members, in short, teamwork. But having fun?

What has fun got to do with being in the military? According to Lucier, fun is the "glue that holds the other pieces together." Under Lucier's direction, the cadets of the Wolverine Battalion certainly know how to laugh: at life's absurdities as well as at themselves. Observed during a recent Dining In, a military tradition, five different groups presented humorous skits about life in ROTC. The underclassmen tweaked the noses of upperclassmen, and upperclassmen did the reverse on the new pledges. Both groups, however, took plenty of shots at the supervisory officer corps. All of the officers took it in good stride. They know, after all, that satire is a form of flattery. Most important, they know they have connected and are making a strong impression on the development of future officers.

The military has always recognized that when you are asking troops to risk their lives for their unit and their country, you had better recognize they are people first. This belief is more and more evident in today's Army. Lucier is a product of the huge transformation the Army underwent after Vietnam. He served under commanders who were veterans. Their emphasis was on preparation, something they felt was lacking in Vietnam. As Lucier explains, their attitude was: " 'I was a platoon leader or a company commander in Vietnam. I remember the soldiers I served with and I remember the leaders I served. [Those soldiers] didn't understand the war, and they didn't want to be there. They weren't ready for combat. I'm not gonna let that happen again."

Inculcated with an ethic of preparedness, effective commanders do not live by documents alone. They lead with their eyes—by looking around to check conditions on the base. Second, they lead with their ears: they ask questions. Third, they lead with their conscience. Lucier explains: "A lieutenant asked me, 'Sir, as a new lieutenant what's the most important thing for me to do?' I said, 'You've got to know your soldiers.' "

Knowing your soldiers extends beyond pleasantries. It's knowing everything about a soldier that will provide a context for his life as a soldier. Lucier elaborates, "It's knowing that Joe is married, Joe has two children, Joe's wife works, Joe has had some financial problems in the past. That's why Joe's wife works and Joe has to take his two kids to childcare at six a.m." As a result, Joe may be late in reporting for duty, a cause for disciplinary action. A good officer will not jump all over a soldier like Joe, but examine the situation first, before taking action.

As an officer in Germany, Lucier had a soldier who tested positive for marijuana. By rights, Lucier in his words "could have crushed the guy" but he did not. Years later, he encountered the man, who was by then a civilian. He thanked Lucier for his second chance. The man had become a practical nurse, was happily married, and was doing very well. Know your soldiers.

It's the human side of leadership that Lucier tries to communicate to his team. "You don't ask someone to do something that you personally can't do yourself." For that reason, Lucier says that an officer must exemplify the military culture in word, thought, and deed. That includes personal fitness. "If you're not willing to do it then don't ask somebody else to do it."

Lucier regards the professionalism of the military as one of its greatest assets. "Underlying the civil military tradition of our nation is the understanding that what I am doing I am doing for my nation. My obligation is to support and defend the Constitution of the United States." That support, says Lucier, is not to a person, nor a position, but to a document that "embodies our national values."

Leadership Partnership: Officers and Noncoms

As part of the ROTC training, young cadets will have to learn to deal with their senior noncommissioned officers, men and women who may have a decade or two of service under their belts. There is no better example of a noncom officer than Master Sergeant Kevin Robinson, a twenty-year-plus combat veteran. "My job is to not only train the freshmen, but to impart my experiences in the Army, and to let them understand [that] as up and coming lieutenants they will have to form a workable relationship with the senior noncommissioned officers."

The role of the noncom in many ways is like that of a factory foreman; they serve as the liaison between management (officers) and hourly (soldiers). It's a delicate balancing act, but one that Robinson knows well. "A new lieutenant coming in is almost like a new soldier coming out of basic training because they know some, but they don't know it all." The noncom's job is to help transform the newly minted lieutenant into a practical military leader. For Robinson, the officer must be willing to do three things: listen, be trained, and understand his role in the relationship.

Toward that end, Robinson says, "I give him guidance on what the unit is doing. What is expected of him as a lieutenant, and how he needs to relate to that platoon sergeant who has fifteen or sixteen years in, and how he shouldn't be intimidated by that sergeant." Robinson cautions young officers that noncoms will try to run a platoon, but it is their responsibility to set the tone for the leadership. The lieutenant, like the noncom, must strike a balancing act that respects the noncom for his leadership, but at the same time, exerts control.

Military history emphasizes the need for a commander to know his troops. Says Lucier, "The history of warfare is that every battle tends to be won and every great strategic action tends to be won by infantry men, the tank commander, the field artillery crew, at the lowest level. Success results from the courage and readiness of the small unit."

For this reason, training is integral to the Army way of life. "If you train for combat," says Robinson, "that training will serve you well." Robinson's training received its greatest test when he served as a sergeant in Lebanon. "Yeah, it'll be scary sometimes, when somebody's shooting at you, but based on the training that you have received, a well-trained soldier will perform."

Habits of Leadership

Lucier has hints about how to make leadership happen. "What works the best for good leaders in the United States Army is that when there is a decision to be made, good officers listen to their subordinates." When the senior officers relies upon the advice of his subordinates, it builds credibility. So, when the officer must make a decision contrary to subordinate input, the subordinates will realize that the "boss knows something they do not" and will more readily accept an unpopular decision.

Communications in the military is not some touchy-feely exercise. There is a structural system behind it. Through a series of confirmation briefings, the commander issues the missions. At the close of the briefing, the commander asks each of his officers: "What's my mission?" It will be up to the officers to explain it, and then elaborate as to how they will fulfill their mission. During a brief-back exercise, the officers explain to the commander how they will accomplish the mission. In this way, there is a two-fold outcome: one, communications are ensured; two, the troops in the field provide the means and the method. In corporate jargon, they are "empowered" to do their mission. Furthermore, the brief-back offers everyone the opportunity to learn what everyone else is doing. In this way, the officers can resolve conflicts over objectives and resources as well as discover any gaps in the planning process.

Lucier received a first-hand education in this process during a stint at Fort Irwin in California where he served as an observer/controller of war game simulations. The troops who emphasized personal initiative, i.e., on-the-spot evaluations, on-site problem-solving, and swift decision-making, were the troops that won the games. Those that relied too heavily on orders from the top, including verification for orders, were those paralyzed in the heat of the battle. In other words, if you have to ask when, where, and how you can shoot, you will be toast!

Leadership Standards

One way officers can exert leadership is to set high standards, and keep them high. For example, Sergeant Robinson believes passionately in what is known as the "hard right." A hard right is putting what is right and necessary ahead of what is easy and convenient. To overlook the details may make an officer or noncom popular, but it may put soldiers in danger. For example, if an officer does not keep his troops current with their weaponry or their fitness, then accidents can occur either later in training, or in combat. "When we make mistakes," emphasizes Lucier, "people die."

Standards are essential to military leadership, but they come alive in the example of those who are in command. "We're there to lead soldiers, to train soldiers," Robinson says. "When we drop the standard, they drop the standard. And we can't have that. When I step out in front of cadets, or in front of soldiers, they're looking at me." For this reason, Robinson does what he can to embody standards in his personal and professional career. [After serving with the Wolverine Battalion for one year, Robinson was promoted to Sergeant Major and moved to the 3rd Army Headquarters, Fort McPherson, Georgia.]

Teamwork also ensures that standards are met. Soldiers are taught to work together to help one another overcome deficiencies. Officers work to channel peer pressure in positive directions to help the strengths of the group overcome the weaknesses of the individual. When this occurs, the unit comes together and a bond of trust forms. The military refers to this bond as "unit cohesion" and it is fundamental to successful military operations. Soldiers are trained to follow orders and standards, but in the heat of combat, when confusion clouds perspective, it is unit cohesion— soldier helping soldier—that keeps soldiers together in times of personal risk and jeopardy. More personally, unit cohesion is the spiritual glue that binds one soldier to another. When you strip away everything else—command, mission, and objectives—it is unit cohesion that makes one soldier put himself in harm's way to preserve the safety of a fellow soldier. Developing and fostering unit cohesion is rooted in military tradition, and it is the duty of every officer to ensure that it flourishes amongst the soldiers under his or her command.

Leadership Training

Lucier grumbles that some university administrators take a dim view of the ROTC program; their attitude is that "it does not teach anything." Lucier counters that the men and women in his program are learning at a very early age how to plan, communicate, delegate, and resolve conflicts—all vital attributes of leadership. Most importantly, these young men and women are putting their skills into practice and that is where the real leadership develops.

Lt. Kuniyuki believes that ROTC works hard to build leadership skills. "Your best hope is that during the four years you can mold [the cadets], and build a good leader, regardless of their background, or personal goals, or intentions. When they leave the program, they'll be capable Army officers."

The other great training ground for officers is, of course, West Point. Major Wayne Doyle, now in the Army Reserves, is a West Point graduate who teaches at Michigan's ROTC program. He believes both systems have their strong points. "I think you learn more about the Army at West Point because you're totally immersed in it," says Doyle. "The product you get at the end, a West Point lieutenant versus an ROTC lieutenant, is very comparable. Both officers are extremely capable. I think having both programs is a good thing for the Army. It creates a little bit of friendly competition." To Doyle, who returned from eight months in Kosovo in March 2000, the two traditions also prevent the development of one way of doing things; both programs have their place.

And here's where the human touch comes in. Lucier believes that officers must learn from one another—good and bad. Upon graduation, the ROTC cadets will be thrust into real-live situations where they will have to deal with enlisted troops, some older, some younger, and many much more knowledgeable and experienced. Young officers also will be dealing with the personal problems of their troops—marital conflicts, financial troubles, illicit drugs. It is demanding stuff for anyone, particularly a fresh-faced twenty-two-year old junior officer.

But it is absolutely essential to learn to deal with those problems right from the start. Leadership in the military often comes down to the basics. As Lucier explains, it is an officer "getting up in front of 200 people and telling them to move from point A to point B." Such a task is easy to envision, but difficult to make happen unless you have some sort of leadership skills.

And it is precisely for that challenge that the Army develops its people—whether it is moving a single person from one point to another, or an entire division overseas—leadership is the ingredient that makes logistics and technical competence flow together seamlessly. Leadership is the sacred trust that binds soldiers to commander, and soldiers to soldiers. It is what makes the Army go in peacetime and in war. Leadership, above all and for all.

ELEANOR JOSAITIS
Leadership in Depth

If you were to pass her on the street, you likely would not look twice. Of slight frame and graying hair, she looks very much her station in life: a mother of five and a grandmother of many more. But if you pause and look into her eyes, you will peek into her soul.

If you have the opportunity to shake hands with her, you will not soon forget the experience. Though she seems not much over five feet tall, the grip of her handshake rings with the strength of an ironworker. And once she has your hand, she does not let go. She draws you to her and looks into your eyes as a kind of soul-to-soul exchange.

By title, Eleanor Josaitis is the Executive Director of Focus: Hope, one of the most extraordinary social services organizations on the planet. By right, she is the spiritual heart and soul of Focus: Hope. Though if you pressed her, she would immediately defer to her 800 colleagues, the many thousands of volunteers, and of course the thousands and thousands of beneficiaries. She cares nothing for titles, honor, or prestige. What she does care about is people. Providing those who have not had an opportunity to reach—as she puts it—the "financial mainstream" of America.

In the wake of the calamitous riots that roiled Detroit in 1967, she and Father William Cunningham founded Focus: Hope as volunteer organization. As Eleanor recalls: "It was actually the day after the riot ended that Father and I walked the streets together and said what are we going to do? We've got to do something right now. And we began right then." Their first effort was an emergency food center.

The mission of Focus: Hope is direct, but its intention is inspirational: "Recognizing the dignity and beauty of every person, we pledge intelligent and practical action to overcome racism, poverty and injustice. And to build a metropolitan community where all people may live in freedom, harmony, trust and affection. Black and white, yellow, brown and red from Detroit and its suburbs of every economic status, national origin and religious persuasion. We join in this covenant."

Personal Mission

The early days of Focus: Hope exacted a personal toll. Eleanor and her husband, Donald, made the decision to move their family, including five children, to an integrated neighborhood in the city. The decision was met with revulsion by her family. Her mother hired an attorney to take her children from her. To combat their resistance, Eleanor strove to be a "perfect mother" to her five children ranging in ages from three to eleven. "I never wanted anybody to criticize me about the way the house was kept, so I would get up at four in the morning. The laundry was always done. The grocery shopping was always done. The house was always neat and orderly. Nobody could ever criticize me that I wasn't taking care of my family." Today she chuckles that all of the time juggling is "probably what made me an organizer."

Donald shared her commitment. As a proprietor of a hobby store, "My husband contributed to this organization when we didn't have a nickel. It was him that always got it started. He's not involved with the running of the organization in any way, but he certainly has always supported me." And so Eleanor held fast to her beliefs. "I learned that you can accomplish more by just rising above it and letting [your opponents] make fools of themselves." Within six months, Eleanor and her mother reconciled. "My mother became my staunchest supporter."

Focus: Hope Today

Located in the heart of Detroit's Westside, an area that three decades after the riots is scarred with abandoned houses and broken glass-strewn streets, the 40-acre urban campus of Focus: Hope stands as testament to what well-intentioned people can accomplish, even when the odds are stacked against them. Since its formal inception in 1968, Focus: Hope has grown to become a nonprofit corporation of 800 full-time employees and more than 50,000 of volunteers with an operational budget exceeding $60 million.

The crown jewel of Focus: Hope is the Center for Advanced Technologies (CAT), which offers associate and degree programs in manufacturing engineering. CAT's manufacturing operations provide parts and services for leading automotive and supplier operations. The Machinist Training Institute teaches apprentices to be tool and die makers. Placement rates for both centers is 100%.

Both are housed in a futuristic looking manufacturing facility that features a series of doors and elevators that can only be opened through hand-touch sensors. A reception area overlooks the entire center; it is called the "Bridge" in honor of Father Cunningham's love of *Star Trek*. Looking from the bridge over the hum and gleam of computer-controlled machinery and a spotless environment, it is hard to imagine that only a few years ago, the place was nothing more than an abandoned factory with natural sky lighting, provided by the holes in the roof. [Success in manufacturing has spurred Focus: Hope to launch an Information Technologies Center to train entry-level and working professions in the expanding worlds of information technologies and their management.]

It is easy to be impressed by the quality and scope of the CAT, but that would be to overlook the network of human and social services that are the real heartbeat of Focus: Hope. These services provide childcare for students and volunteers, food programs for the community, and educational programs to help students complete high school and GED requirements as well as a foundation for entry into the technical programs. As their mission states: we pledge intelligent and practical action. Those actions take form in the interlocking network of food, support and educational services that makes Focus: Hope unique among social service providers.

Creating Opportunity

The operative concept of Focus: Hope is opportunity: opening an avenue for clients to enter the "financial mainstream."

"When you have a job, you can buy a house," says Eleanor. "You can buy a car. You can be part of the community. You don't have to go and stand in somebody's food line. You can educate your children. You can have self respect and dignity."

The spiritual heart of Focus: Hope is perhaps the food center. More than 40,000 people receive some food assistance through its programs. But the manner of dispensing food is different. "People are treated with dignity. They're not handed a box of food," explains Eleanor. "They push a shopping cart. They take the items off the shelf themselves." In this way, patrons of the food program will feel better about themselves. And if they have children with them, they will not be embarrassed by the perception of taking a handout. This emphasis on humanity is reinforced a thousand ways throughout the organization. From the logo of black and white hands locked in a handshake to the smiles of the people who work or volunteer, the spirit of human affirmation permeates everything and everyone.

But Focus: Hope is not about giving things away; it is about creating a community where people make for themselves. Students must remain drug-free as well as commit to regular attendance; they also pay their own way. [Tuition grants, however, are readily available from a variety of private and governmental sources.] As an example, every student in the Machinist Training Institute first makes a set of tools. To purchase the tools would cost $700. To make them personally is priceless. "Can you imagine how they feel walking out of the door knowing, I did this? It's a sense of pride," Eleanor avers.

Eleanor relates another story from a student whom she gave a lift home. When Eleanor asked why he was wearing his uniform (most students leave them at work), he said, " 'Mrs. J., when I used to go into the bank I was nothing. Now when I go in there, they'll say, 'Oh you're over at Focus: Hope. You're studying to be an engineer?' Then I am somebody.' " Eleanor concludes, "It's those little tiny things that make all the difference in a person's life."

"Race has excluded a lot of people from opportunities. When we started the Machinist Training Institute, we interviewed 487 shop owners. Only two had ever hired a minority, or a woman." As a result of receiving training, Focus: Hope graduates broke barriers and entered job markets from which they had previously been excluded.

Eleanor is firm in her personal mission for Focus: Hope. "I want the organization to be the very best in the world," she says. "And then what do I want to do? I want to share it with everybody." The sharing is evident in many visitors from around the country as well as the world who come to Focus: Hope to learn the lesson of how to create, as it says in the mission statement, a metropolitan community where all people may live in freedom, harmony, trust and affection.

Driven by Spirit of Volunteers

Throughout those years, Focus: Hope has served as the nexus between people in need and people asking: "What can we do next?" In a sense, that is the question that Focus: Hope has been answering for more than three decades. Eleanor firmly believes that people want to help; they simply need to be asked. And she is not shy about asking.

One of her most notable recruits is Lloyd Reuss, the former president of General Motors. Reuss now serves as the executive dean of the Center for Advanced Technologies. He credits the organization with teaching him that often the only thing missing from urban youth is opportunity.

"If you provide opportunity, they will do well." As he put it in a recent interview, "For thirty-eight years I worked at shaping steel. Now I am shaping lives." [1]

It is for this moment of personal recognition that whenever business and government leaders visit Focus: Hope, Eleanor insists that they meet and greet staff and students. "They're going to brag because they shook hands with the president of the corporation or Colin Powell. Those small little moments give people pride and dignity."

And the opportunities for meeting and greeting are plentiful. Focus: Hope also has become a favorite stomping ground of politicians and business leaders. Presidents Bush and Clinton have visited. As chairman of the Joint Chiefs of Staff, General Colin Powell made a telling remark to an assembled organization. "You people blow me away." His simple statement reflected the overwhelming sense of awe that visitors feel when they visit Focus: Hope because they can feel the energy and spirit of the organization. Eleanor makes the most of these contacts. In her cause for civil rights, Eleanor has become proficient at communicating her message to those who maneuver the levers of power; she is passionate in her support for nutrition programs for children and the elderly, as well as for educational programs for urban youth.

The Organizer

For most of the first three decades of Focus: Hope, it was Father Cunningham who was the public face of the organization. As Eleanor puts it, Cunningham had the gift of preaching, so it was only natural that when this fledgling organization began, it was Cunningham who should be front and center. "He was a master communicator. I was a master organizer."

In her naturally deprecating style, Eleanor says she was a housewife and unfamiliar with the limelight. But she and Cunningham were a team. Together they shaped the vision for the organization. While Cunningham served as the voice of conscience as well as chief fundraiser and cheerleader, Eleanor worked behind the scenes to make certain things got done. The two of them made all key decisions jointly, as well as debated them vigorously. Staffers believe it was from those give-and-take debates that Focus: Hope gained the strength it needed to hold to its mission in the face of opposition.

When Father Cunningham was stricken with cancer in late 1996, Eleanor was asked to assume his leadership role. But she kept him abreast of everything through daily visits to his bedside. She also took him for visits to Focus: Hope. "I wanted him to see what progress was being made." At their last visit, he made a request. "'Eleanor, do not put my name on this boulevard and do not name a building after me. Make my work live on.'"

Skeptics outside the organization might have assumed that the death of such a charismatic leader such as Father Cunningham might have crippled an organization. But anyone who knew Eleanor understood that such talk was nonsense. Those who know her have looked into her eyes and felt her hands. There is strength founded on firm faith and a passion for what is right and moral.

Origin of Commitment

From where does Eleanor's strength emerge? "I was always a very faith-filled person, from the time I was a small child. I went to a Catholic grade school and high school, and I always believed in the Gospel. The Gospel message is so simple: 'Love one another as I have loved you.'" Eleanor shakes her head as she reflects, "Just why do we make it so complicated?"

Eleanor had known racism since childhood. She recalls a childhood scene that occurred during Detroit's infamous race riots in 1943. She heard neighbors using racial epithets as they angrily condemned the actions of the black rioters. "I was a child hearing this nonsense, but it made an impression on me, and I thought, this is so silly. We've got to change this."

Her commitment crystallized much later. As a young adult she recalls watching the drama *Judgment at Nuremberg* on television and its being interrupted with newsreel images of police wielding cattle prods and fire hoses against civil rights demonstrators in Selma, Alabama in 1965. The juxtaposition of the recreated drama and the actual drama was traumatic. "The little kids [in Alabama] were flipping over in the air, and people were running and throwing their hands above their head. I cried my eyes out [watching]. I kept saying, what is the difference between what went on in Germany and what's going on in my country? It changed me. And I challenged myself to say, 'What am I doing about it?'"

Leadership in Depth

Eleanor and Father Cunningham made plans for the future with a concept Eleanor calls "leadership in depth."

"For any leader to be successful you have to have people around you that understand what the mission and the purpose is and are willing to take on the leadership role to make that happen," says Eleanor. "There isn't just one person. None of my colleagues left when Father announced he was going into the hospital. None of my colleagues left when Father passed. That says something about the leadership of the organization and their belief in what my vision for the organization is."

Reuss, the former GM executive, credits Eleanor with making an effective transition to the front-and-center position of leadership. She knows she must adjust to a world of continuous change and she is doing a good job of pushing Focus: Hope. Eleanor in turn praises Reuss for teaching her to adapt to change as well as a sense of patience. The two speak openly and frequently about all of the issues and challenges facing Focus: Hope. Reuss also has counseled Eleanor when to back off "when I want to jump in and take something over myself because it's not moving fast enough." As she says, "Lloyd is my mentor, my friend and my colleague."

Personal Style of Leadership

Today Eleanor works to extend the concept of leadership in depth by being available both as an executive and a mentor. This openness is evidenced by her office. It is in the middle of the floor, with no walls separating her from the ebb and flow of the business of the day. "I want people to see me, to come in and interrupt me, to ask me questions, or to introduce me [to others]."

As befits her style, Eleanor is everywhere throughout the organization. Every Tuesday at 7 a.m., she meets with new colleagues joining Focus: Hope. At these sessions, she discusses the early days of Focus: Hope as well as the current challenges the organization faces. These meetings are her way of communicating the lessons of the past as well as an opportunity to invigorate the vision of Focus: Hope for the next generation. People who join the organization do so because they are motivated to make life better for others. When they meet Eleanor, they gain insight into a woman who has made Focus: Hope's mission of recognizing the dignity and beauty of every person her life's work. From Eleanor, they share in her energy as well as her practical approach to getting things done with determination and, yes, dignity.

Reflection

Eleanor uses her early mornings for reflection. Up before dawn, she spends a half-hour or more each day thinking, praying and reflecting. She also reflects in another way. Although she lives within six-minute drive to her office, she never drives the same way to work. "I will drive fifteen miles out of my way to take a different route every day."

What she does on her many different routes is look at the urbanscape of her city, looking at the homes, the parks, the schools, and shopping centers—imagining possibilities for what is there now and what might be there in the future. But it is the people who engage her deepest attention, for example, the young woman waiting at the bus stop at 5:45 a.m. with her two kids in tow. Looking at the scene, Eleanor wonders about the circumstances that compel a woman to rise so early and be obliged to bring her young children along. It is small dramas like this that shape Eleanor's commitment to her mission. Grateful for the "options" in her own life, she wants Focus: Hope to create options for others. And it is those options—food, childcare, education, and jobs—that lie at the core of Focus: Hope. "The work that we're in demands the creativity, the values, and the persistence of every single one of us. Civil rights is not child's play."

The Light Touch

One of the ways that Eleanor keeps spirits up is through her keen sense of humor, often at her own expense. Once when she was rattling off arcane technical details about a co-generation power project Focus: Hope was working on with a noted manufacturer, her daughter caught her up with the line: "'Mother, who are you kidding? You can't even change the bag in the vacuum cleaner.'" Eleanor chuckles, "You know, your kids keep you grounded." As can her staff. At times, Eleanor can seem the taskmaster. When this occurs, staffers say that she is riding broom, as in witch's broom. So to celebrate the thirtieth anniversary of Focus: Hope, the staff pitched in and made her an electric broom, complete with seat and handlebars. Eleanor loved it. "I might not know how to change the bag on the vacuum cleaner, and I might not know everything about co-generation, but I know how to surround myself with people who do. And I think that's what a leader has to do."

Natural Disaster

She would need all of her leadership skills to cope with the disaster the struck Focus: Hope shortly after Father Cunningham died. A tornado touched down and inflicted $18 million worth of property damage. "You want to talk about tenacity, a tornado can give you tenacity real quick." Within hours, the staff along with volunteers had gathered and was busy at work moving offices to a building down the street. The organization never lost a beat; social services and the school continued. "The team was here in minutes and that's leadership in depth," says Eleanor. In some ways, the tornado may have served Focus: Hope well. Not only did the organization benefit from some new construction, the disaster demonstrated publicly Eleanor and her team's fortitude, resiliency, and grace under pressure.

The Future

The future of Focus: Hope will require the skills of the next level of leadership, men and women who already are moving forward in new and different ways. And that's the way of the organization. Eleanor challenges her managers: "I want your ideas. I want your mind. I want your leadership. So every single manager who runs any part of this organization is a leader, and that's what I want to create. I want to create leaders that go out of here and create other leaders."

Ask how she would like to be remembered and Eleanor is quick to respond. "As a woman who had a passion for civil and human rights and made a difference, and a woman who had a strong faith in God."

Like her partner, Father Cunningham, Eleanor needs no monument to her memory. Her memory will remain strong in the hands she has gripped and the souls she has stirred to a good cause. Her legacy will live on in the tens of thousands of lives that Focus: Hope has touched. And as Eleanor will say, it is not what Focus: Hope does for an individual, it is what it enables individuals to do for themselves, opening the door for opportunity. Or as its name says, for hope. No leader could hope for a better legacy.

Acknowledgements

I have had the pleasure of working with men and women in leadership positions for more than twenty years. Throughout the years, I have gleaned much from their experience. Their insights into leadership have helped me form my own ideas about what it takes to be a leader.

In writing this book, I have been helped by a great many people. First, I want to thank all of the individuals who agreed to allow me to interview them about their leadership styles. Their patience with my questions, at times unformed, is a testament to their individual leadership characters.

Next, I want to thank some folks at Ford Motor Company for their special assistance. Chuck Snearly, Chris Vinyard, and Ed Miller were gracious with their time and insights. John Spelich, formerly at Ford and now at Gateway, was another big help.

Tom Ufer was a special pal who opened some doors at Michigan for me. His brother, Bob Ufer, graciously allowed me to pepper him with questions about his leadership experiences in sports management and law. Stew Nelson and Rocky Pozza made some additional connections for which I am grateful.

I also want to thank some pals in the writing business. Nick Kober was in my corner the whole way urging me onward. Tom Morrissey provided critical support. Al Lee guided me through the minefields of getting a book to press. Chris Merlo helped keep my calendar booked. And Chuck Dapoz was the book's unofficial cheerleader.

I owe a special thanks to five other colleagues: Dan Denison for challenging me to write my own ideas about leadership; Sandra Penkalski and Mike Weiss of Imageweaver Studios for providing insights and graphic know-how; Eric Harvey for delivering guidance at critical junctures; and Kathy Macdonald for sharpening my perspective on first-time leaders.

And then there were my friends who patiently listened to my progress reports. These include Angela and Rich Robben who cheered me on and Matt Derrenberger who always asked, "When's the book coming out?"

And, of course, very special thanks goes to my mother-in-law, Monica Campanella, whose combination of patient support and willingness to play games with our children, Paul and Annie, enabled me the extra time I needed to finish this book.

And most of all, I want to thank my wife, Gail Campanella, the love of my life, who typed the interviews, corrected my many mistakes, and kept this book on track.

Thank you all!

N OTES
Part 1

PROLOGUE

1 McKenna, Regis *Real Time: Preparing for the Age of the Never Satisfied Customer.* Boston, MA: Harvard Business School Press, 1997.

CHAPTER 1

1 Eisenhower, Dwight "Noteworthy Quotes" *Strategy & Business* Issue 8 Third Quarter, 1997.
2 Burns, James MacGregor *Leadership,* New York: HarperCollins, 1979.

CHAPTER 2

1 McCullough, David "Harry Truman" from *Character Above All.* ed. Robert A. Wilson. New York: Simon & Schuster, 1995.
2 Badaracco, Joseph L. Jr. "The Discipline of Building Character" *Harvard Business Review* March–April 1998.
3 Badaracco, Joseph L. Jr. "The Discipline of Building Character" *Harvard Business Review* March–April 1998.
4 McCullough, David "Harry Truman" from *Character Above All.* ed. Robert A. Wilson. New York: Simon & Schuster, 1995.
5 Fisher, Anne "Test: Can You Laugh at His Advice" *Fortune* 7/6/98.

CHAPTER 3

1 Mission Statement, Focus: Hope, Detroit, Michigan.
2 Bennis, Warren & Nanus, Bert Leaders: The Strategy of Taking Charge. [Cited in Hitt, William D. *Thoughts on Leadership: A Treasury of Quotations.* Columbus, Ohio: Battelle Press, 1992.]
3 Drucker, Peter The Practice of Management. [Cited in Hitt, William D. *Thoughts on Leadership: A Treasury of Quotations.* Columbus, Ohio: Battelle Press, 1992].
4 Senge, Peter M. *The Fifth Discipline: The Art and Practice of the Learning Organization.* New York: Doubleday, 1990.
5 Sanders, Betsy *Fabled Service: Ordinary Acts, Extraordinary Outcomes.* San Diego, CA: Pfeiffer & Company, 1995.
6 de Geus, Arie *The Living Company.* Boston, MA: Harvard Business School Press, 1997.

CHAPTER 5

1 "Gone Fishin'" *Business Week* 6/22/98.
2 Warsaw, Michael "Keep It Simple" *Fast Company* Vol. 15 June/July 1998.
3 Warsaw, Michael "Keep It Simple" *Fast Company* Vol. 15 June/July 1998 [CNN Survey].
4 Lowe, Janet and Welch, Jack *Jack Welch Speaks: Wisdom from the World's Greatest Business Leader,* San Francisco: John Wiley, 1998.

CHAPTER 6

1 Tichy, Noel "The Mark of a Winner," *Leader to Leader* No. 6 Fall, 1997.
2 Kittrell, Ed "Funny Business" *American Speaker: Your Guide to Successful Speaking* July/Aug. 1997.
3 Powell, Colin and Persico, Joseph *My American Journey.* New York: Random House, 1995.

CHAPTER 7

1 Stewart, James B. *Den of Thieves.* New York: Simon & Schuster, 1991.
2 Shellenbarger, Susan "Employers find it isn't costly to keep workers happy" *Wall Street Journal* 11/19/97.

CHAPTER 8

1 Gordon, Judith R. *Organizational Behavior,* Fifth Edition. Upper Saddle River, NJ: Prentice Hall, 1996.
2 Gordon, Judith R. *Organizational Behavior,* Fifth Edition. Upper Saddle River, NJ: Prentice Hall, 1996.
3 Gardner, Howard *Frames of Minds: The Theory of Multiple Intelligences.* New York: Basic Books, 1983.
4 Gibbs, Nancy "The EQ Factor" *Time* October 2, 1995.
5 Goleman, Daniel What Makes a Leader? *Harvard Business Review,* 76, (6) 1998.
6 Lapides, J. "The Adult Learner" [Course Notes on Motivation adapted from McClellan, D.] University of Michigan, Dearborn, 1998.
7 Langer, Ellen J. *Mindfulness.* Reading, MA: Addison-Wesley, 1989.
8 Gardner, Howard *Leading Minds: An Anatomy of Leadership.* New York: Basic Books, 1995.

CHAPTER 9

1 Sullivan, Gordon R. and Harper, Michael V. *Hope Is Not a Method.* New York: Times Books, 1996.
2 Ambrose, Stephen, "When Was the Real Techno-Revolution?" *Fortune* 12/2/96
3 Kurtzman, Joel "An Interview with Gary Hamel" *Strategy & Business* Issue 9 Fall, 1997.
4 Senge, Peter M. *The Fifth Discipline: The Art and Practice of the Learning Organization.* New York: Doubleday, 1990.

CHAPTER 10

1 Senge, Peter M. *The Fifth Discipline: The Art and Practice of the Learning Organization.* New York: Doubleday, 1990.

2 Barker, Joel Paradigms: *The Business of Discovering the Future.* New York: Harper-Collins, 1992.

3 Hammer, Michael and Steadman, Steven A. "The Power of Reflection," *Fortune* 11/24/97.

4 Hammer, Michael and Steadman, Steven A. "The Power of Reflection," *Fortune* 11/24/97.

5 Sullivan, Gordon R. and Harper, Michael V. *Hope Is Not a Method.* New York: Times Books, 1996.

6 Moore, Hal and Galloway, Joe *We Were Soldiers Once...And Young.* New York: Random House, 1992.

CHAPTER 11

1 Gardner, John W. On Leadership. [Cited in Hitt, William D. *Thoughts on Leadership: A Treasury of Quotations.* Columbus, Ohio: Battelle Press, 1992].

Notes
Part 2

Jac Nasser

1 Naughton, Keith "Ford's Global Gladiator" *Business Week* 12/11/95.
2 Simison, Robert L. "Ford Decides to Teach Workers New Idea: 'Shareholder Value'" *Wall Street Journal* 1/13/99.
3 Wetlaufer, Suzy, "Driving Change: An Interview with Ford Motor Company's Jacques Nasser" *Harvard Business Review* March–April, 1999.
4 Simison, Robert L. "Ford Decides to Teach Workers New Idea: 'Shareholder Value'" *Wall Street Journal* 1/13/99.
5 Simison, Robert L. "Ford Decides to Teach Workers New Idea: 'Shareholder Value'" *Wall Street Journal* 1/13/99.
6 Zesiger, Sue "Jac Nasser is car crazy" *Fortune* 6/22/98.
7 Blumenstein, R., Simison, R., and White, J. "With Rivals Ascendant, GM Feels Urge to Hasten Drive for Efficiency" *Wall Street Journal* 6/12/98.
8 Shaw, Robert "Passion for the Business: An Interview with Jacques Nasser" *Leader to Leader* Number 12, Spring 1999.
9 Lapham, Edward "Rip up the org chart, Nasser declares (interview) *Automotive News* 11/22/99.
10 Zesiger, Sue "Jac Nasser is car crazy" *Fortune* 6/22/98.
11 Lapham, Edward "Rip up the org chart, Nasser declares (interview) *Automotive News* 11/22/99.
12 Zesiger, Sue "Jac Nasser is car crazy" *Fortune* 6/22/98.
13 Zesiger, Sue "Jac Nasser is car crazy" *Fortune* 6/22/98.
14 Zesiger, Sue "Nasser Speaks Out" *Fortune* 9/18/00.
15 Simison, Robert "For Ford CEO Jacques Nasser, Damage Control is 'Job One'" *Wall Street Journal* 9/11/00.

Red Berenson

1 Thomaselli, Rich "U-M Hockey, Berenson Stands for the Right Things" *Ann Arbor News* 4/2/98.
2 Thomaselli, Rich "U-M Hockey, Berenson Stands for the Right Things" *Ann Arbor News* 4/2/98.
3 Pitts, Antoine "U-M Hockey Posts Memorable Decade" *Ann Arbor News* 12/29/99.
4 Thomaselli, Rich "U-M Hockey, Berenson Stands for the Right Things" *Ann Arbor News* 4/2/98.

JILL KER CONWAY

1 Conway, Jill Ker *Road from Coorain*. New York: Alfred Knopf, 1989.
2 Libman, Norma "Sheepish no longer" *Chicago Tribune* 1/1/95.
3 Conway, Jill Ker *Road from Coorain*. New York: Alfred Knopf, 1989.
4 Rotenberk, Lori "A lady lets her hair down" *Chicago Sun-Times* 5/4/98.
5 Conway, Jill Ker *Road from Coorain*. New York: Alfred Knopf ,1989.
6 Rotenberk, Lori "A lady lets her hair down" *Chicago Sun-Times* 5/4/98.

SKIP LEFAUVE

1 McGrory, Mary "The Ringers of Saturn" *Washington Post* 11/29/92.
2 Brown, Warren "What if you had a party and 28,000 Saturn owners showed up?" *Washington Post* 6/26/94.
3 Aaker, David A. "Building a brand: the Saturn story" *California Management Review* 1/1/94.
4 LeFauve, Richard G. "Getting Results While Keeping Your Soul" *Leader to Leader* No. 9 Summer 1998.

DAVID MCKINNON

1 *Success* August, 1994.

RICK SNYDER

1 Fricker, Daniel "Snyder has made a lifelong habit of success" *Detroit Free Press* 7/17/98.
2 Davis, Dwight "Speaker cites keys for business" *Ann Arbor News* 2/23/00 [Quotes in this paragraph come from this article].
3 Fricker, Daniel "Snyder has made a lifelong habit of success" *Detroit Free Press* 7/17/98.
4 Anderson, Scott "Tech fund could be city's hook" *Ann Arbor News* 10/26/00.

WOLVERINE BATTALION

1 Sullivan, Gordon R. and Harper, Michael V. *Hope Is Not a Method*. New York: Times Books, 1996.

ELEANOR JOSAITIS

1 Sittendorf, Curtis "Hope is a weapon" *Fast Company* Issue 22 March, 1999.

NOTES
Chapter Heading Quotes

PROLOGUE

Fitton, William Ed. *Leadership*. Boulder, CO: Westview Press, HarperCollins, 1997 [Quote from U.S. Army publication].

CHAPTER 1

Heider, John *The Tao of Leadership: Lao Tzu's Tao Te Ching* Adapted for a New Age. Humanics, 1985.

CHAPTER 2

Wooden, John and Jamison, *Steve Wooden: A Lifetime of Observations and Reflections On and Off the Court*. Lincolnwood, IL: Contemporary Books, 1997.

CHAPTER 3

Van Ekeren, Glenn *Speaker's Sourcebook II: Quotes, Stories & Anecdotes for Every Occasion*. Englewood Cliffs, NJ: Prentice Hall, 1994 [Quote by Robert Schuller].

CHAPTER 4

Mintzberg, Henry "Noteworthy Quotes" *Strategy & Business* Issue 8 Third Quarter, 1997.

CHAPTER 5

Griffith, Joe *Speaker's Library of Business of Stories, Anecdotes & Humor*. Englewood Cliffs, NJ: Prentice Hall, 1990 [Quote by Peter Drucker].

CHAPTER 6

Boone, Lewis E. *Quotable Business: Over 2,500 Funny, Irreverent, and Insightful Quotations about Corporate Life*. New York: Random House, 1992 [Quote by Henry David Thoreau].

CHAPTER 7

McCormack, Mark H. *What They Don't Teach You at Harvard Business School*. [Cited in Gomes, Helio Quality Quotes Milwaukee, WI: ASQC Quality Press, 1996].

CHAPTER 8

Goleman, Daniel "The Emotional Intelligence of Leaders" *Leader to Leader* Number 10 1998.

CHAPTER 9

Gomes, Helio *Quality Quotes.* Milwaukee, WI: ASQC Quality Press, 1996 [Quote by Heraclitus].

CHAPTER 10

Hitt, William D. *Thoughts on Leadership: A Treasury of Quotations.* Columbus, Ohio: Battelle Press, 1992 [Quote by Soren Kiekegaard].

CHAPTER 11

Fitton, William Ed. *Leadership.* Boulder, CO: Westview Press, HarperCollins, 1997 [Quote by David Ogilvy].

SUMMARY

Fitton, William Ed. *Leadership.* Boulder, CO: Westview Press, HarperCollins, 1997 [Quote by Vince Lombardi].

Index

About the Author

John Baldoni has been meeting the communication and management development needs of organizations large and small for more than 20 years. His clients range from Fortune 500 companies such as Abbott Labs, Albertson's, Ford Motor Company, Gateway and Kellogg's to entrepreneurial start-ups. John consults at the University of Michigan and is a frequent lecturer and speechwriter on leadership topics. In addition, John is the author of dozens of articles on leadership as well as the book, *180 Ways to Walk the Leadership Talk*. For more insights into the art and practice of leadership, visit John's website at www.LC21.com.